LUTHER CHRISTMAN:
A MAVERICK NURSE -
A NURSING LEGEND

Dr Elizabeth Pittman

TRAFFORD

USA ▪ Canada ▪ UK ▪ Ireland

Note for Librarians: A cataloguing record for this book is available from Library and Archives Canada at www.collectionscanada.ca/amicus/index-e.html
ISBN 1-4120-6833-9

Printed in Victoria, BC, Canada. Printed on paper with minimum 30% recycled fibre. Trafford's print shop runs on "green energy" from solar, wind and other environmentally-friendly power sources.

TRAFFORD

Offices in Canada, USA, Ireland and UK

This book was published *on-demand* in cooperation with Trafford Publishing. On-demand publishing is a unique process and service of making a book available for retail sale to the public taking advantage of on-demand manufacturing and Internet marketing. On-demand publishing includes promotions, retail sales, manufacturing, order fulfilment, accounting and collecting royalties on behalf of the author.

Book sales for North America and international:
Trafford Publishing, 6E–2333 Government St.,
Victoria, BC v8t 4p4 CANADA
phone 250 383 6864 (toll-free 1 888 232 4444)
fax 250 383 6804; email to orders@trafford.com
Book sales in Europe:
Trafford Publishing (uk) Limited, 9 Park End Street, 2nd Floor
Oxford, UK oxi ihh UNITED KINGDOM
phone 44 (0)1865 722 113 (local rate 0845 230 9601)
facsimile 44 (0)1865 722 868; info.uk@trafford.com
Order online at:
trafford.com/05-1744

10 9 8 7 6 5

Contents

PROLOGUE

by Luther Christman

My career as a nurse, administrator and academic has involved many concerns that to go to the heart of nursing, its identity and image in the minds of faculty, nurses themselves and the public it serves.

Many of the issues that face nursing have not yet been resolved. Debates are still going on regarding, for example: the level of education for entry into the profession; which level of preparation is best for the provision of optimal care; the advantages and costs of a primary nursing over the team nursing model; and the desirability of faculty being practicing nurses.

This biography recounts the part that I have played in bringing these issues to the forefront in the minds of the profession. And the ways in which I have tried to demonstrate ways of resolving these through the introduction of organizational and educational changes in the institutions in which I have served.

Importantly, the biography deals with the prejudice that male nurses still encounter to this day. Discrimination plagued my own career and although I reached positions of considerable authority in nursing, in the end it prevented me from totally achieving some the improvements to nursing which I hold most dear. I believe it is time that the subject of discrimination against men in a female dominated profession is discussed, acknowledged and dealt with. I have proposed a system of affirmative action for the profession that has served women in male-dominated professions well, but needless to say the proposal has fallen on deaf ears. I certainly hope this account of my career will not only raise discrimination as an issue, but will help to prevent its continuation. We need more men in nursing. The recurrent shortages of nursing staff has reached crisis point in most English speaking countries and men are a largely untapped source of new entrants into the profession. The American Assembly for Men in Nursing, of which I am president, is working towards recruiting and supporting men. It is an uphill battle; changing the widely held belief that nursing is a woman's profession takes time and patience.

This biography is the outcome of interviews and lengthy correspondence with the author, Dr Elizabeth Pittman. Biographers are always interpreters as well as storytellers. Her interpretation of the events in my early history and professional life are very close to my own. An Australian academic, her thorough research has enabled an objective analysis of what I have tried to achieve in the United States nursing arena.

Luther Christman PhD RN, 2003

PREFACE

My introduction to Luther Christman came about when I was writing a master's program on leadership in nursing. I had been searching the literature for a nurse whose career demonstrated strategic thinking, and while there were a number to choose from, my preference was to have someone who Australian nurses were unlikely to have previously studied. A colleague, Professor Alan Pearson, suggested Luther Christman. After reading all I could find about his career, I thought that postgraduate students would find the topic more interesting if more details of the challenges he had faced as a leader were included. In 2002 I wrote to him and, to my surprise and delight, his response was 14 pages long. This was the beginning of a fruitful correspondence that is still going on. Christman is a good raconteur and as more details of his career unfolded and his trials as well as his achievements became apparent I became convinced that here was a story that should be told. I asked him if anyone had written his biography and was extremely pleased when he took up my offer to do just that.

In October 2004 I stayed with Luther and his late wife Dorothy at their home in Tennessee for a very busy week comprised of daily interviews and research in his private archives. Luther proved to be a charming man, generous with his time and a very good host. Then it was on to Boston for another week since a great deal of other archival material is held in the Mugur Library at Boston University.

As this biography will show, Christman's illustrious career places him as one of the most remarkable nurses of the 20th century, yet he has also been one of the most controversial. His vision for the improvement of the nursing profession entails a critique of its organization, policies, practices, education and female domination that challenged nursing leaders, physicians and hospital administrators alike. A very vocal protagonist, he campaigned on many fronts—most notably for a single education level for nursing registration and the integration of education and practice. He did not win every battle and some of the issues he tackled have still to be resolved.

As a white, Anglo-Saxon, Protestant, heterosexual family man Christman does not belong to a group that is normally associated with social prejudice. Yet, early in his nursing career, he faced discimination because he was a male in a predominantly woman's profession. Eventually Christman hit a glass ceiling. It was the most blatant public example of gender discrimination he ever faced, and as well as being a great personal disappointment, it was one that limited his influence in nursing affairs.

Nevertheless by the time he retired in 1987, Christman had become a nursing icon. Thoughout his career Christman has had appointments that were the first of their kind. He was the first male to be appointed a dean of nursing. He was also the first nurse to be appointed a dean of nursing and a director of nursing at the same time (Vanderbilt University and Vandebilt Hospital respectively). Later on Rush Medical Center and University repeated this kind of joint appointment when he became vice president of nursing affairs and dean of the college of nursing.

Christman is now one of the most honored and awarded and internationally recognised figures in American nursing. He has not only received most of the highest accolades and awards that nursing can bestow, his contribution to scholarship and practice has been recognised by medicine and many other disciplines.

One of the first nursing honors Christman received was that of Outstanding Male Nurse in the Nation. The National Association of Male Nurses in 1975 gave him this award before Christman became actively involved and the organization changed its name to the American Assembly for Men in Nursing. He received the Council of Specialists in Psychiatric and Mental Health Nursing award in 1980, and the Honorary Recognition Award from the Illinois Nurses' Association in 1987 and the Jesse M. Scott Award by the American Nurses' Association followed in 1988.

Although Christman retired in 1987 he is still receiving awards. In 1992, the Center for the Advancement of Nursing Practice, Beth Israel Hospital, presented him with the History Makers in Nursing Award. In honor of the work Christman did to advance clinical practice, education and administration, Grand Valley Strand University presented him with an honorary doctorate in 1998. The University of Detroit gave him a Distinguished Nurse Scholar award in 1999 and when a Catholic priest made the announcement, it tickled Christman's wry sense of humor: 'Fancy a Catholic University giving an award to someone named Luther!' The Tennessee Nurses' Association added their Lifetime Achievement Award in 2002, specifically mentioning his work to increase diversity in nursing at Vanderbilt, where he was the first to employ African-American women as faculty and actively recruit men into nursing. The same year, both the Golden Lamp Society, Rush University and the American Association of Critical Care Nurses added to the long list of nursing honors and awards that are too numerous to mention in their entirety.

Of all the nursing organizations that have honored him, it is Sigma Theta Tau awards that he seems to value most; they have acknowledged his scholarship and creative thinking. Sigma Theta Tau, the nursing honor society, admits nurses of scholarly stature who have made a significant contribution to the profession and Christman was admitted to this august society in 1964. In 1981, the society awarded him the Edith Moore Copeland Founders' Award for Creativity; he was the third nurse to receive this distinction. Gamma Phi Chapter of Sigma Theta Tau recognised his contribution to nursing with the first annual Mentor award in 1986. Then in 1991, Sigma Theta Tau, International (STTI) recognised his contribution with the first Lifetime Achievement award. The cover of a 2002 edition of STTI's journal *Reflections on Nursing Leadership* featured his photograph. The journal ran a seven-page article describing Christman's achievements. That year he was admitted to the American Nurses Hall of Fame, the first male nurse to receive this honor.

Nursing is not the only discipline to recognise Christman. In 1972, the Institute of Medicine, National Academies of Sciences, made him a Fellow. Two years later, the Institute of Medicine, Chicago, made him a Fellow in recognition of his work at Rush University. Seven years later he was made an honorary life time member by Alpha Omega Alpha (the medical honor society) for his advancement of clinical nursing throughout his career—the only nurse to be recognised in this way. In 1982, the American Association for the Advancement of Science made him a Fellow. This latter award is a prestigious acknowledgment of the quality of Christman's research and innovations in nursing and only one other nurse has received this honor.

The scientific community conferred other fellowships and honors. In 1961 he was admitted to Alpha Kappa Delta, Sociology Honor Society in recognition of his sociological research. The Society for Applied Anthropology was the first to make him a Fellow (1972) in recognition of his research in the field of anthropology.

Honorary doctorates followed as his career advanced. The Thomas Jefferson University of Philadelphia conferred a Doctor of Humane Letters (1980) for Christman's advancement of the nursing profession. In 1985 he was made an Old Master of Purdue University, which selects two to five brilliant scholars from various disciplines who subsequently lecture to a multidisciplinary audience. The Strand Valley State University bestowed an Honorary Doctor of Science, 1998.

Christman's career is redolent with unusual and sometimes humorous stories of events in American nursing. It certainly has its high notes despite the discrimination he suffered and the controversy that his campaigns engendered. In the end the profession that put so many barriers in his path has deemed him one of their Living Legends. Now a retired, sprightly 90-year-old, he reviews books for the American Journal of Nursing, is president of the American Assembly for Men in Nursing and is still a provocative advocate for his vision of nursing.

This biography could never have been written without the generous whole-hearted support of its subject, Luther Christman. The same may be said of his colleagues, Faith Jones and and Shirley Fondille—both gave me interesting insights into Christman's management style. Joan LeSage and other colleagues from Rush Medical

Center and University generously provided material about Christman's administration and leadership during his term there.

Since my retirement in 2002, I have been very fortunate to have an adjunct position in School of Nursing and Midwifery, Faculty of Health Sciences, La Trobe University. This appointment has allowed me to concentrate on writing this biography. I am extremely grateful to both Professor Stephen Duckett, Dean of the Faculty and Bill Maguiness, Head of the School, for their support.

All authors need the help of readers who patiently read through drafts and offer comments and criticisms and I am no exception. In this regard I am deeply grateful to Luther Christman, to Betty Rankin, a retired Australian nurse, to Ann Woodruff, retired head of a school of nursing, to Faith Jones, a colleague of Luther's, and to Julie Pittman, my daughter-in-law. Julie, who is not a nurse, willingly agreed to report on whether the drafts were understandable to someone outside the profession.

Behind every woman author there should be a director of support services to keep the household running with a minimum of fuss. My husband Ian Pittman very generously took on this essential role and his cheerful support is very gratefully acknowledged.

Elizabeth Pittman BA(hons) MEd DEd FRCNA

CHAPTER ONE

CHRISTMAN'S FIRST CAMPAIGN

On 8 December 1941, President Franklin Delano Roosevelt announced that the United States of America was at war. The shock caused by the bombing of the fleet at Pearl Harbor was so great that young men rushed to enlist in the armed services. Caught up in the fervor to serve the nation in a time of war, Luther Christman, a 24-year-old nurse, penned a letter to the Surgeon General offering to serve at the front lines in the Army Nurse Corps for the duration of the war. His offer was refused. The US Army would not allow men to serve in the Army Nurse Corps.

The refusal was based on a 1901 law that had established the Army Nurse Corps. The law specifically stated that army nurses were women, despite the fact that in the previous century only men attended wounded soldiers. Although a large percentage of the few qualified male nurses volunteered for service in World War I, most served as foot soldiers and were not given the opportunity to practice their profession. So when Christman volunteered to serve as a nurse in

World War II, he was very disappointed but not really surprised when his offer was refused.

The army only allowed male nurses to serve as non-commissioned orderlies. Even this position carried a 'catch twenty-two'—they were considered too qualified to go to corps school and without doing that they could not function as orderlies. Therefore during World War II they were assigned to duties that had nothing to do with health care. One registered nurse, Private Jacob Rose, eventually learnt to drive a truck and fill in potholes in the roads. He did that for most of his term of service. Neither his nursing skills nor those of five other male registered nurses he knew were used. Yet the army was crying out for nurses and was expending large sums on advertising urging women nurses to volunteer.

The irony was that the paternalistic attitudes of the times meant that women nurses were barred from serving on the front lines, so they were confined to base hospitals. Doctors were so busy in the base hospitals they did not serve on the front lines either, although not explicitly barred from doing so. This meant that the wounded could not receive immediate emergency nursing care before being transferred to the base hospitals for medical attention. Christman thought that if the army accepted male nurses, they could give front-line care and stabilize the injured ready for transportation. The letter he sent to the Surgeon General has been lost, but in part it said:

> You may be aware that men nurses are not accepted by the armed forces into their nurse corps. We men nurses feel that this discrimination is unjust and unwarranted. During this crisis the armed forces should avail themselves of our skill and experience. If given the opportunity we are able and willing to serve to the best of our ability.[1]

The exclusion of trained male nurses suited most nursing leaders who saw nursing as the one profession where women could predominate. Army nurses themselves were against admitting men because they feared men would take over the officer positions.

In 1942, a bill had been passed giving nurses regular officer status including equal pay. Officer status was very important. Since injured men came from all ranks, including officers, without the rank of officer nurses would lack sufficient authority to carry out their duties. Given that the army was a male-dominated conservative institution, it was not surprising that army nurses thought that if men were commissioned, they would immediately replace women officers. In practical terms these fears were unlikely to be realized—at that time male nurses represented less than half a percentage of the total nursing workforce.

Christman believes that the 'snide' response he had received from the Surgeon General was most likely written by 'some nurse in the Army Nurse Corps—but nevertheless he [the Surgeon General] signed it. ... His curt, condescending letter had in no way responded to my offer'.

'As a young enthusiastic and outraged citizen' Christman says he was determined to take a stand. Even though he was a young, recently graduated nurse working in a predominantly female profession, he decided to campaign to get men admitted to the Army Nursing Corps. The campaign was based on the idea that the U.S. government and public would want their wounded service men to receive the most immediate and appropriate care that could be given. To drum up support Christman sent copies of his letter, plus the Surgeon General's response, to every United States Senator and about three-quarters of the members of the House of Representatives. The point he had chosen to make had wide public appeal and evoked an enormous response. As the letters came in, it was clear that most government members supported the campaign and only a few were opposed to men serving as nurses. Christman says:

> My first support came from Senator Taft, the leading Republican in the Senate and was followed almost immediately by that of Senator Wagner, the leading Democrat. General Dwight D. Eisenhower wrote offering strong support. Colonel Mayo complained bitterly about the ruling that men, who were nurses, could not be used in any role that cared for the sick and injured. But the two top physicians in the Pentagon firmly opposed me.

Members of each political party put forward reasons for the exclusion of men that fitted their party's political agenda. The Democrats claimed that the Pentagon was wasting an opportunity. Some Republicans wrote to say that President Roosevelt's New Deal was to blame. Despite such partisan views, about two-thirds of the House of Representatives wanted to commission men.

The press became involved. A *Saturday Evening Post* editorial questioned the policy of not using male nurses in the war. Both the *St Petersburg Times* and the *Christian Science Monitor* (a well-respected newspaper with a wide readership) ran similar articles supporting Christman's position.

By this time, to avoid being drafted to serve in a non-nursing post, he had joined the United States Maritime Service. He was assigned a position as a 'Pharmacist's Mate, First Class', a post which at least bore some relation to his training. At first his pharmacist mates laughed at his campaign, but the laughter ceased as letters of support came pouring in. Maritime officers expressed support, but doubted he would succeed, given the entrenched conservatism of the Army.

Secretaries offered more practical support, volunteering to remain after hours, take dictation and type Christman's letters.

The Pinnella County District Nurses' Association was the only nursing organization to publicly endorse Christman's stand. An army nurse roundly criticized the Pinnella Association. She said that if men nurses were admitted they would replace women army officers. Christman says that the American Nurses' Association opposed his campaign. But in 1946, LeRoy N. Craig (head of the nursing school where Christman had trained and who supported his efforts) maintained that the American Nurses' Association had actually supported his stand.[2] In Craig's view, the real reason behind the exclusion of men was that the Surgeon General himself did not believe male nurses should be commissioned—a view that appears to have some substance. As the United States entered the war, at the request of the Men Nurses' Section, the American Nurses' Association had written to the Surgeon General requesting that male nurses have equal opportunities to serve. The reply by the Acting Surgeon General of the Medical Department revealed the army's conservative attitude:

> I regret that this office cannot concur in your opinion. It would be impracticable to employ male nurses in times of peace since such employment could complicate unnecessarily the administrative problems. We feel we have provided satisfactory and dignified positions for such male nurses as may be employed during the military emergency. In addition, we feel that the Secretary of War would not approve the legislation suggested by you.[3]

Christman's campaign and the resulting publicity did bear fruit. The Surgeon General was called before several committees related to the war effort to explain why male nurses were not allowed in the Army Nurse Corps. Worried by an apparent shortage of women nurses, the Surgeon General introduced a bill to draft women. Regardless of party differences, senators across the board assured Christman that no women would be drafted until the supply of male nurses was exhausted. At last there was a chance for the issue of male nurses to be raised and discussed, but just as the bill was about to be debated by Congress, the Battle of the Bulge occurred in Europe and the impending defeat of Germany became apparent. The nurse draft bill was dropped and all efforts to commission men as nurses were abandoned. Of the 1200 male nurses who did serve in the war, most were given posts quite unrelated to their profession.

The social attitudes of the 1940s meant other groups had been excluded from serving. It was not until 1941 that the Army admitted black nurses. Given the prejudice against blacks in that era, they were probably not seen as a threat to the white nurse officers; in any case, a quota was imposed on the number that could be admitted. Women doctors were another group who experienced similar discriminatory practices in both World Wars.

In World War 1, army officials actually said that the words 'person' and 'persons' in their regulations did not include women—the words meant man or men! So the American Medical Women's Association sent a petition to the Surgeon General against the gender discrimination inherent in the regulations. The petition was unsuccessful—no woman doctor was commissioned. Instead 55 women doctors were contracted to perform surgery in European hospitals without 'military status or benefits such as pensions or military bonuses'.[4]

In the second World War, women doctors again faced gender bias. By this time, unlike male nurses, women doctors did have their own separate professional body through which they could effectively lobby—the American Medical Women's Association. They also gained some support from feminist groups. Not surprisingly, state medical societies (predominantly male) refused to back them on the grounds that a woman's place was on the home front. This time, like Christman, the women doctors grounded their campaign on an appeal to the general public. They maintained that the need for adequate surgical care of the wounded should prevail. During congressional hearings, they pointed out that the army sent male obstetricians abroad but left the most skillful female plastic surgeons at home. Eventually in 1943, the Sparkman-Johnson Bill was signed into law and women doctors were admitted to the Army and Navy Medical Corps. By garnering wider support the women doctors' efforts had a much more immediate result than Christman's lonely battle.

Although Christman's campaign was successful in generating some congressional support and in publicly raising the issue, it had failed in its main objective. It was not until after the Korean War that the law was changed and men were admitted to both the Army and Navy Nurse Corps. Ironically the bill to permit male nurses to serve as officers was put forward by a woman. Frances Bolton from Ohio was then one of only seven women to be a member of the House of Representatives.[5] Bolton had long been an advocate for nurses. It was Bolton who successfully instigated the bill that enabled female nursing officers to have equal rights and status with male army officers. A woman with strong views on fairness and equity, her later bill effectively eliminated the discrimination against males serving as nursing officers. By the time the United States became involved in the Vietnam conflict, 500 male nurses were providing care for the injured. Today more than 30 per cent of the registered nurses in the Military Nurse Corps are men.

This episode is the first of many strong stands Christman was to take throughout his controversial and often militant career. The campaign to admit men to the Army Nurse Corps carried a personal risk. He had already experienced discrimination on account of his gender and, given the position taken by female army nursing officers, he knew his stand could have damaged his career prospects. As the story of his youth shows, determination and the need to succeed are characteristics that developed early in his life.

CHAPTER TWO

GROWING UP

The young nurse who had the nerve to take issue with the US Army was born in 1915. The second son of Elmer and Elizabeth, Luther was the eldest of the four Christman children who survived childhood. Albert, their first born had convulsions and died shortly after his birth. Two other children failed to survive infancy; one was born with spina bifida and the other contracted pneumonia. Luther's two sisters, Eleanor and Lois Kathryn, and his young brother Elmer Junior were the other survivors.

Luther's childhood was spent in Summit Hill, a small mining and farming town in Pennsylvania. Summit Hill was not as isolated as some country towns were at that time. Its railway connections made it a tourist venue for the well to do. An underground fire in the seams of coal was one attraction. It burnt for 100 years, despite the one million dollars spent on concrete piles driven 300 feet deep in efforts to extinguish it. Steam and smoke that gushed up at points along its trajectory were actually all that could be seen, which may have disappointed sightseers. The other attraction was the switchback railway operated by a stationary steam engine and gravity. The 12 passenger carriage was connected by steel cables from the engine house to the Barney car which pushed it uphill. Here gravity took over and the carriage ran down the slope and then glided up to the terminus in Summit Hill at a cost of 50 cents for the round trip. In 1920 the mine owners billed it as the most wonderful 18-mile ride on the continent.

The well-to-do tourists were noticeable in a town populated by a variety of religious and ethnic groups, most of whom were poor by comparison. In the twenties and thirties, Summit Hill had a population of about 5,500 people clustered together according to their European origins or religious affiliations. The Catholics (40 per cent) lived in one part of the town and the Protestants (60 per cent) in the other. There were six churches in the town and religious divisions among the townspeople were evident. Political allegiance emphasized these differences—most Catholics voted Democrat and most Protestants voted Republican. There were two schools for children from any origin and one for Polish immigrants while the Catholics had their own parochial school system. As far as Christman remembers there were no black families and only one Jewish family in the town.

For most of Christman's early years his family lived where the houses of two main religious groups converged. The Protestant Christman household was on one side of the street and a Catholic household was directly opposite on the other. As a boy he came to know many individuals in the various groups through mixing with other boys and his job selling newspapers and periodicals. He thought most of townspeople were very nice despite the deep religious and ethnic differences that separated them and as a young lad he came to the conclusion that religion could be very divisive:

> I abolished organized religion in my mind at about 15
> years. I discussed this with some of my teenage friends
> and later with the clergyman who was such a big help
> to me. He wanted me to become a clergyman like him,
> but I explained that I couldn't. I had become very cyni-
> cal about organized religion because of people fight-
> ing each other just because they did not go to the same
> church. At that time people thought I was an odd ball.

Early awareness of Summit Hill's social and religious differences
did not cloud Christman's appreciation of its other attributes. He
loved the countryside, the feeling of serenity, the sweep of the rolling
hills, the sharp peaks and green valleys. Even as a young boy, living
on a plateau gave him a sense of vision and curiosity and his interest
was stimulated by the changes that the seasons brought to the trees,
flowers and habits of the animals. His mountain rambles meant he
could be alone with his thoughts, and sketch or write poetry. The
winter climate was severe with snowstorms and an average of three
feet of snow on the ground. One of young Luther's joys was trudging
to school through the snow wearing hip boots:

> I enjoyed going to school in the hip boots I had to wear
> because of the snow. I used to strut around in these hip
> boots. The other kids only had galoshes and that kind of
> stuff. Since I was the shortest and thinnest in the class,
> the boots made me feel powerful. I had to be more ag-
> gressive to keep up with the others.

Growing up in the midst of the Depression in the USA, Christman saw that many of the town's families lived in near poverty.
He says that although his family never had to worry about having
enough to eat, there were no luxuries and few recreational activities.
Strict religious observance on Sundays meant the Christman chil-

dren were not allowed any play activities other than reading on those days. A trip to another town was considered an exciting event. Each year his family would take the long seven-mile journey to visit relatives in Nesquehorning (named after the Indian tribe slaughtered by the whites) and stay over night. Although tourists came to Summit Hill by train, the main transport for the inhabitants was horse and buggy or streetcar, but mostly they walked everywhere. It was young Luther's mountain walks that gave him a way of escaping the troubles of his family life.

Luther's mother, Elizabeth Christman was not well liked by the residents in Summit Hill. A brusque and outspoken woman, she made enemies more easily than friends. Many members of the extended family lived in Summit Hill, including Luther's paternal grandparents who were originally Pennsylvanian Dutch, with German ancestry several generations back. None of these relatives invited his mother into their homes. He says that everyone avoided her and can only remember his mother having one friend. Her unpopularity was not surprising given that she believed her religion was superior, and she freely expressed her political allegiances. According to her, Methodists, of which she was one, were viewed as sacred—everyone else was a pagan. She particularly despised Catholics and she did not hesitate to let them know she disliked their religion. In Elizabeth Christman's view only those who voted straight Republican in every election were good citizens—the rest were un-American. She was a fervent member of the Ku Klux Klan[i]. Although the Klan was notorious for their treatment of blacks, in Summit Hill the Ku Klux Klan

---

i. Although the Ku Klux Klan originated in southern states, it spread to northern states including Pennsylvania. The Klan included both women and men among its members. It not only targeted Blacks—the Klan were also against Catholics, Jews and any other 'foreigners' who were not white Protestants (Chalmers, 1965).

targeted Catholics and Christman remembers them burning crosses in the Catholic area from time to time.

Young Luther's boyhood was bedeviled by a very poor relationship with his mother. He says:

> My early years were nightmarish. My mother was very cruel and brutal. The least deviation on my part from what she thought was right (and she was never wrong) caused a whipping. At first she used my father's leather razor strop. Later she had my father make a cat-o-nine-tails, which she used instead. I was constantly in pain. I clearly recall one incident when I was about five years old.
>
> Buster Brown shoes for children were the rage and I desperately wanted a pair and finally my father bought me a pair. I was so excited and proud, I raced across the street to show the two sisters, unmarried Catholic women, who lived opposite. One was a schoolteacher and the other a stenographer. They were so pleased with my happiness. When I returned home, I received one of the worst beatings of my life—I could hardly stand erect while my mother yelled at me for daring to associate with Catholics. I don't know how I survived the abuse as well as I did.

His worst affliction was the cat-o-nine tails—the razor strop was far less painful. Although as a child he had no alternative but to submit, the abuse finally drove him into action. One day when his mother was shopping and his father was at work, he went to the family outhouse and dropped the homemade cat-o-nine tails in the contents of the pan.

Fortunately Christman came from tough stock—on his maternal side a number of relatives lived to 100 and one even to 104 years. Like all children before the advent of antibiotics and immunizations he contracted most of the common childhood infections. Since there was neither prevention nor treatment, only the strong survived measles, scarlet fever, pneumonia and diphtheria. A diphtheria epidemic in the town claimed the lives of two of his young friends and for Luther it was a close call. His sleeping quarters were in the attic—a very cold place in winter. One morning he was weak and feverish with diphtheria and did not get out of bed. His mother stormed into the attic to find out why he was not downstairs doing his chores, and found him too weak to stand. A doctor attended him every day after that but in those days the only real treatment was the body's natural defenses.

His father, Elmer, although a good-hearted man, was dominated by his wife and he failed to intervene in her treatment of their oldest son, so young Luther was unsure of his father's love. That is revealed in a remark Christman made about the time that his widowed father came to stay with him and his wife Dorothy.

> After my mother died my father opened up to me and I realized he adored me—he told everyone that when he came to stay with Dorothy and me.

His father's life was one of hard work. He too, had had a difficult mother who took all of her sons out of school at age ten, sending them to work in the mines of Summit Hill. The boys picked out the slate from the coal as it came up from the mine. Elmer was considered a good worker and by the time he married he had risen to be an electrical foreman in the Leigh Navigation Coal Company, although he had no formal education in this field.

After a mine cave-in, Elmer was out of work for six months with a fractured skull. Then he got a job on the trolley cars as a conductor. Eventually motor cars made the trolley cars redundant. After he fell and badly injured himself during a snowstorm he retired and became the caretaker of the Methodist Church until he suffered a heart attack and died in his seventies. Apart from the short periods following accidents, Elmer was never out of work during the Depression years. Christman attributes this to his father's reputation as a good worker and his easy-going friendly personality and he says he never heard a negative word spoken about his father. An active parishioner in the Lutheran Church, Elmer was on the board and at one time a treasurer. He was a member of the Knights of Malta[ii] and the Summit Hill Rod and Gun Club. As Elmer aged he played the role of Santa Claus in a major department store in a town near Summit Hill, and parents invited him to visit their children dressed in his Santa's garb. Since Elmer was obviously a popular and respected man in the community—the contrast between the two parents could hardly have been sharper.

Elizabeth and Elmer attended different churches—she was a Methodist and he was a Lutheran. The separation in religious observance symbolized their relationship; they seldom did anything together. Christman describes his mother and father's marriage as more like a business relationship than a marriage:

> My mother ran the house with a heavy hand, she took all my father's money and she did all the spending. She and my father did not share a bedroom—my father slept in part of the attic. If divorce had been an

---

ii. The Knights of Malta was formed by monks and for a time was a fighting force. Now groups with allegiance to the original precepts have been formed in numerous countries of which the USA is one.

option at that time they would have been divorced. She got tremendously overweight. She just sat and ate and became a diabetic. She broke with her family tradition (most of whom were centenarians) by dying in her sixties. Nobody missed her much. Very few people came to the funeral. I was living at Michigan but I went to her funeral—I went for my father's sake.

Although Elizabeth Christman was unfriendly and abusive to his sisters Eleanor and Lois Kathryn, she did not beat them. Nor did she treat her other son, Elmer Junior like she treated Luther. Naturally, Luther often wondered why he was the only child that was so abused by his mother. Describing the events that preceded his mother and father's marriage, he reached a conclusion that must have made the abuse more bearable:

A few days before my mother was to be married to another man, he jilted her and almost immediately he married another woman from the community in which they all lived. My mother had been dating this man since she was sixteen and she started working in a silk factory. She was just crazy about him. As a young boy I met him several times and he was big, handsome and very athletic looking. At the same time my father was dating a woman who was very personable from all accounts. They planned to marry. But she contracted pneumonia and died suddenly shortly before the wedding. Both my parents had these experiences at around the same time, although they did not then know each other since they lived in towns 10 miles apart. They met when my father was visiting my mother's town. After discovering the similarities in their experiences, they started dating and in a couple of months they married. I don't think the marriage ever satisfied my mother.

My mother's previous fiancé and his wife came to visit our house occasionally. Even as a youngster, I was startled by the difference in her behavior in this man's presence. She was charming, neatly dressed and her conversation was pleasant. She was always glancing at him with an adoring look. Her behavior to this man seemed like that of a lover. This was quite different to the way she interacted with my father. She even treated insurance agents and other salesmen that came to the house more graciously than she treated him.

When I got older I came to the conclusion she had married my father for financial support, since in those days most women couldn't find employment. I concluded that I must be a symbol of a marriage she did not really want. I was the first living child that had made divorce impossible. All her anger was focused on me. I drew this conclusion as a teenager. That was when I stopped talking to her. From when I was about 12 years old we only spoke when it was forced on us—when she came into the room, I went into another.

Although family relationships were not quite so fraught with difficulties for his two sisters, they escaped as soon as they could. Eleanor was 18 months younger than Luther and she left home when she was 15 years old and lived with a first cousin of their mother's in Philadelphia. Unfortunately the cousin was an alcoholic and Eleanor started drinking too. Eventually she developed Alzheimer's disease but the basic condition contributing to her death was alcoholism. Christman had a close relationship with Lois Kathryn, the youngest and now the only surviving sibling. Lois Kathryn also left home as soon as she could and entered a hospital school of nursing. She married a man of Polish descent who discouraged contact with people other than Poles and her relationship with Luther lapsed, but after she became a widow it was renewed and they still keep in touch.

His brother Elmer was the only child to whom his mother showed any real affection. She babied Elmer Junior in a way that the youngest child, Lois Kathryn, was never babied. Such favoritism must have seemed unfair. Christman says he often fantasized that, even though his brother was named after their father, Elmer Senior was not Elmer Junior's real father.

Elmer Junior had a charming personality like his father and everyone liked him. As a young lad Luther had to take Elmer Junior with him everywhere he went and he grew very fond of his brother. In WW2, Elmer Junior was drafted and sent to a Pacific island, where he picked up a rare virus, which damaged his heart. He had heart surgery in one of the big hospitals in Philadelphia that was quite successful. Then about 20 years later Elmer Junior needed surgery again. At that time Christman was at Rush Medical Center where there were some very successful heart surgeons, who, in Christman's opinion, were far more qualified and experienced than the one Elmer Junior was attending. Elmer Junior died soon after his operation, and the real affection that Christman felt for his brother is evident in the deep regret he still feels because he was unable to persuade him to change surgeons.

As a young boy Luther turned to his maternal grandmother, Mathilda Barnicot, for motherly warmth and affection. His grandmother was a tolerant caring woman. Her guiding star was the 'golden rule' and Christman says it became the central concept in his own life. She and her Cornish husband had settled in the township of

Nesquehorning after they married. As a widow (her first husband died before Christmas was born) she took positions as a housekeeper, often living with the families who employed her. Mathilda had cooked for royalty before her marriage and her skills as a cook were well known, so she gained employment at a time when there were very few jobs for women. While waiting for a live-in housekeeping position, she sometimes lived with the Christmans in Summit Hill. Eventually she married again, this time to John Leonard, the superintendent of a zinc processing plant in Palmerston, Pennsylvania. He was a kind, gentle and thoughtful man who, knowing young Luther's interest in the natural world, subscribed to the National Geographic Magazine.

His grandmother's gentleness was an antidote to his mother's abuse and they spent many hours together when Christman stayed with her and his stepfather during summer holidays. Both of them expressed confidence in his abilities and encouraged him to be a good student so that he could have a career.

Another early positive influence in life was the books by Horatio Alger. The stories were about poor boys that overcame all their obstacles to become adults of some responsibility. Christman felt inspired by the stories and says they helped him deal with his troubled relationship with his mother and his early difficulties at school.

Six was the age at which every child started school in Summit Hill. At his mother's insistence, Christman started school when he was four years old even though this was against the rules. Christman remembers being with her when 'she accosted the school principal in a loud and nasty manner'. Under the pressure of her attack, the superintendent reluctantly agreed to take her son at this young age. His mother wanted him to graduate when he was 16 so he could start earning immediately—a point she reiterated throughout his school days.

Two years younger than his classmates, Luther's early school years were really tough going. Since he was the youngest and smallest he could not compete in the sports activities, he became the butt of the other boys. Practically all the other boys had gone to kindergarten so they had a head start in reading and writing. He remembers that: 'The second grade teacher was very hard on me because I couldn't keep up'. By third grade Luther had started to get abreast of the others and the teachers left him alone. But his problems were not over, for during his primary school years, his mother's constant vocal disdain of Catholics brought another problem in its wake.

In the sixth grade he scored 98 per cent in mid term, but his report card only showed 88 per cent. He talked about this with his father, who decided to see his teacher, who was also the school principal. The principal was a Catholic who lived in the same street as the Christmans and, like most of the people in the town, was well aware of Elizabeth Christman's attitude to his religion. Christman could hear the ensuing discussion. In essence, the teacher was saying that he did not like young Luther's attitude so he had dropped his mark by 10%. His father's charm and positive commonsense eventually prevailed and Christman's rightful mark was restored.

As he became more successful at school, he gained the confidence to start writing poetry and his poems were put up on the walls of the classroom. An interest in artwork developed and young Luther decided he would become either a poet or an artist. Once he was in high school he started to achieve scholastically and make friends. His interest in animals and their habits had been stimulated by his exploration of the countryside and the farms in the region, so he took a year of biology. He persuaded his biology teacher to let him show his classmates how baby kittens were formed. Although how babies were made and developed in the uterus was not discussed as openly as it is today, in a farming community it was not such a strange request. Taking a stray pregnant cat, Luther and his teacher gave it a lethal dose of ether. To the fascination of the girls in the class, he opened up its corpse, bringing out the partially developed kittens to show how they were attached and growing.

In senior high school Christman ran into another problem with his grades that was actually the result of a careless clerical error. His records became muddled up with those of his cousin, Fred Christman who, although very good at sports, was no scholar and consistently got poor marks. Their class of 105 was divided into groups based on previous grades which were taken as indicators of each student's scholastic potential. Because of the recording error, Christman's apparently poor grades placed him in the low potential group. It was not until his second year at senior high that the principal discovered the mistake, and he was immediately moved to the top group. This incident led to a close relationship with the principal, Edward McCullian, who realizing Christman's potential gave him a glowing reference when he left school.

Like all boys Christman got into mischief occasionally and he recounts one prank with some amusement and just a hint of triumph:

> The French teacher was one that none of us liked. He was aloof and unresponsive. One night after he and his wife had retired three of us tied a rope from his front door knob round the house to the backdoor knob. In the morning he couldn't leave his house because he couldn't open the doors. He had to telephone for assistance and was late for work, and he never found out who did it.

His high school years were full of activities—Christman was in the band and in all the school plays. The high school plays attracted a big audience. In those days radio was just beginning, there were no talking movies in the town, and television was unheard of, so the plays were a great source of community entertainment. There was usually a full house for each production. Needless to say, his mother never went to see the plays he took part in.

The debating team provided another outlet and no doubt that experience served him well in his later career. He took part in the athletics team becoming quite a fast runner. Fully-grown he was only five feet seven inches, so most of the boys were much bigger and stronger. When they asked him: 'How come you can run so fast?' Luther's wry response was: 'That is my only protection from the rest of you.'

During the Depression years, finding odd jobs was not easy. While he was still at school Christman peddled newspapers and magazines to the various ethnic and religious groups, worked for the baker a few hours a week, and undertook any other tasks that earned him small sums. His mother took any money he earned no matter how small, and gave him a nickel or a dime for pocket money—if he was lucky. Peddling newspapers was the most irksome and least profitable job. He had to walk a long way to pick up the magazines from a town in the valley and carry them back uphill. If he had taken a streetcar it would have cost 15 cents and the Saturday Evening Post only sold for five and sometimes people did not pay him. Selling the magazines did have one advantage, it meant he met many of the people his mother would have forbidden him to mix with.

The scarcity of work during the Depression Years is highlighted by the story of Christman's second job after he finished high school. He had already worked on a Work Project Administration site (part of President Roosevelt's New Deal) but eventually the appropriation money ran out. On the basis of this experience he obtained a job in highway construction. He had only worked a few hours when the manager found out his father was in full-time employment. It was an unwritten rule that families did not have more than one income source in those hard times. He was fired on the spot.

His mother had already approached the Methodist minister about finding a suitable job for Luther. She pointed out that she certainly did not intend her son to stay at home since she had no intention of supporting him. Fortunately by now young Luther had a reputation as a virtuous and personable lad with some leadership potential and both the Lutheran and Methodist ministers had each tried to encourage him to become a clergyman. The Methodist minister, Charles Wesley Bair, offered to support Luther and get him financial aid if he chose to study for the clergy, regardless of which church he chose. Luther refused this offer explaining his objections to organized religion and expressing a preference for an artistic career. Wisely Reverend Bair pointed out that becoming a poet or an artist was not an option in the Depression and he suggested training as a nurse. This suggestion solved several of Luther's problems, although he has always claimed he just stumbled into nursing. It would mean he could leave his troubled home because nursing schools provided accommodation and meals. He could earn while he learnt, an important consideration for a young man with no resources or family support. But Luther said he was only interested if his girlfriend Dorothy wanted to be a nurse too, since they planned to marry once they were earning sufficient money.

Dorothy Black and Luther had started dating in high school. Mostly their dates consisted of long country walks since he had no money to take her anywhere. Every now and then he would get some money together without his mother knowing and take Dorothy to a movie, which in those days cost 35 cents for each of them. Mostly they just walked around Summit Hill from the time Dorothy left Sunday church until dinnertime, at which point Dorothy's father, James Black, would invite him to their home for dinner.

Mrs. Black was a very friendly out-going woman who everyone liked. She knew his mother by reputation so he never had to explain about his difficult home life. Mr. Black was a right-wing Republican and the chief politician in the town and was often out campaigning. When he came home Mr Black would wind up the clock and that was the signal for Luther to leave. Quite obviously the Black family approved of Luther's relationship with Dorothy and since she was keen to continue it, she readily agreed to become a nurse.

Fortunately for Luther and Dorothy, Reverend Bair was a Philadelphian and knew about the Pennsylvania Hospital Nursing School for Men. There was a separate school for women at the hospital but the school required students to pay to commence, which stopped Dorothy from applying there. However the Methodist Hospital in Philadelphia (now merged with the Thomas Jefferson Hospital) offered nursing training to women and required no payment and, on the strength of Reverend Bair's recommendation, Dorothy was accepted as a student.

The move to Philadelphia promised happier times, but was accompanied by a sad event. Christman had a faithful friend in his collie dog, Nellie. Everyone in the town always knew where he was because Nellie was lying there waiting for him. Just before he was to begin his nursing training, the collie developed cancer and Christman knew there would be no one to take care of her in her last days. So he took her out into the forest, shot her and buried her. He knew it was a better kind of death for his dog, but it was a terrible experience that he clearly remembers more than sixty years later.

Although Luther Christman's childhood was beset by harsh treatment and early struggles there were many positive experiences and he grew into a personable young adult well liked by people within his community and the family into which he hoped to marry. Throughout his life nothing would ever seem as bad as the brutal treatment he received in those early years. He says in retrospect: 'My mother was always putting me down and never wanted me to be successful but in spite of that [or because of it] I developed a passionate commitment to succeed.' Commitment to succeed was not the only positive outcome. Christman knew he was a survivor, and it was this knowledge that gave him both determination and courage when faced with adversity later on in his life. As he entered nursing he had no way of knowing just how determined he would have to be to make his way in a woman's profession.

Young Luther Christman

Dorothy Christman - nee Black
(born 1917- died 2004)

CHAPTER THREE

Becoming a Nurse

When Luther Christman became a trainee nurse at the Pennsylvania Hospital School for Men in 1936, all nursing education took place in hospital schools; the first university program did not begin until 1944. The Pennsylvania Hospital School was very different to later hospital schools, both in its setting and in its training. The educational principles and standards reflected the moral and ethical values of the 1930s. To 21st century nurses some of the idiosyncratic criteria for acceptance into the school will seem amazing or even repugnant.

The Pennsylvania Hospital and its school had a long and prestigious history. The hospital was the first to be founded in America. Benjamin Franklin and a Quaker, Dr Thomas Hood, established the hospital in 1751 to care for the sick-poor and insane who roamed the streets of Philadelphia. Dr Benjamin Rush, who became known in America as the 'father of psychiatry', was a member of staff for 30 years. Over a 100-year period the hospital developed into a complex that included maternity and surgical departments, and a separate psychiatric section known as the Institute of Pennsylvania Hospital. In 1885, its newly established nursing school created a precedent— its female graduates were permitted to nurse on both male and female wards. But, in 1908, nursing education became separated by gender and a school for women was started in the general hospital. Then six years later, a separate school for men was established in the psychiatric institute. There, male nurses would be trained to attend male patients. It was the first nursing school to be headed by a man, a nurse by the name of LeRoy N. Craig.[6]

Like similar institutions of its time, the psychiatric section was set in several hundred acres of parkland on what later became prime real estate. When Christman started training there, it was actually a private hospital, where patients paid large fees for their treatment and residency. Hence they were either wealthy or had their fees paid by their church or some other benevolent group. By the first half of the 20th Century, the hospital had gained some renown for its then modern, and sometimes experimental, treatments: such as electroconvulsive therapy (ECT), insulin shock therapy and, a treatment for third stage syphilis. This latter treatment involved injections of blood drawn from patients with malaria in the hope that a high malarial fever would kill the spirochetes that caused the patient's syphilis.[7]

Craig, head of the school in Christman's time, was a man of high ideals and an innovator. Generally, nursing schools for men limited men's training to the fields of behavioral health and male genito-urinary nursing. In Craig's view such programs lacked depth in nursing. Under his leadership, two years of the school's program focused on the treatment of mental illness while the third year was devoted to general nursing. By 1932, the nursing school for men was one of the nine 'diploma', or hospital-based nursing schools, that included both general and psychiatric nursing. Over the years approximately 12,000 students trained at the Pennsylvania school.[8]

On Christman's arrival at the school he presented his reference from the principal of his secondary school which said he was a young man that had always exemplified the highest ideals of American youth. He spent the first two days being interviewed and undergoing clinical psychology tests and assessments and was immediately accepted as a patient attendant until the classes started in eight months time. These eight months was in reality a probationary period, which all prospective students underwent to ensure they were suitable to work with patients. No doubt this practice provided the hospital with a very convenient group of low-salaried, earnest workers. Of the 75 accepted as patient attendants in Christman's group, only 30 were accepted as student nurses.

Christman's class was entirely composed of mature men. He says:

> Now twenty-one—I was the youngest one in the class—others were more mature. One student was a 45 years old engineer who had lost his job during the Depression. Others were younger fellows who had part of a college education but whose families could no longer afford to keep them and who could not get jobs to see them through their courses.

In this time of high unemployment, Craig could pick and choose who was admitted for training. Craig was determined to recruit the 'right kind' of men into the school. He was adamant that nursing was not the right profession for poorly adjusted or inadequate people. The **explicit** criteria for entry were good grades in their previous education and a healthy report from the psychological tests. Reflecting Craig's own middle class background and the prevailing prejudices of the times, the **covert** criteria were evidence of gentlemanly behavior and absolutely no overt signs of homosexuality. Thus, although well intentioned, some of his yardsticks and methods for determining the suitability of candidates appear unethical from a 21st century perspective.

Part of the interview process included lunch with Craig and table manners were closely observed. Crumbs on the table, or any other departures from middle-class table etiquette, meant the prospective student was summarily rejected! Craig, believing that homosexuals did not play sport, thought that emphasizing sporting prowess was a way of eliminating them from the school, so sporting activities were actually part of the curriculum. Since some of the male patients were young adolescents and sport was among the therapeutic activities, student nurses were required to have tennis gear and rackets.

To further ensure that students were heterosexual, their dating habits were observed. Christman was not seen to be dating during his probation—he was waiting for Dorothy to arrive in Philadelphia and take up her place in her nursing program. When Dorothy became ill and Christman requested leave to visit her in Summit Hill their relationship became known and any concern about his sexual proclivities evaporated.

Students were expected to display a high level of moral behavior at all times. This was considered important since home nursing for middle and upper class people was one of the main avenues of nursing employment in the 1930s. Students were expected to supervise their own behavior to some extent and they conducted a 'court' to examine any suspected breaches. Teaching staff obviously supported this activity since several students were expelled on the advice of their peers. Christman cites a variety of reasons for students being expelled, but two clearly display the sexual mores of this time. One student was dismissed on the suspicion of homosexuality and another because of a report about excessive sexuality on a date with a woman. It is scarcely surprising that only eight men managed to stay the length of the program.

Writing in 1988, Christman says it did not take him long to realize that men were a minority in nursing and what being a member of a minority meant. During the general nursing year of his training it was plain that female nurses viewed men with suspicion. The following illustration of this is in Christman's own words.

> One day, while I was scrubbing in the operating room, a young woman needing a cholecystectomy was brought into the room. The surgeon discovered she had a full bladder and ordered a catheterization. The operating room supervisor told me to leave. She said I could not stay because I was a man. When I mentioned that the surgeon was a man and that the surgery would be further delayed if I was forced to leave and then rescrub, she stomped off. After the surgery the supervisor told me I did not understand the role of men in nursing.

> On another occasion, I was called a pervert for answering the urologist's request to examine a specimen under a cystoscope while in the presence of a fully draped female patient and a female nurse.

To be registered as a nurse Christman had to sit an examination in obstetrics so he asked if he could have some clinical experience in an obstetrics ward. The only place he could gain the experience was in the women's part of the general hospital, which was close by, but quite separate from the psychiatric hospital. However, the director of nursing, Miss Helen McClelland refused; she did not want a male nurse in her maternity area.

At the time Christman made his request, the hospital had started a program training taxi drivers, policemen and firemen to assist at births. The program was in response to a public outcry about the number of emergency births occurring in places other than labor wards and without adequate assistance. In those days the policemen and firemen did not even have a high school education and the taxi drivers had even less. He goes on to describe what happened when he requested labor ward experience:

> I submitted a request to the members of the faculty of the school for women. I asked to be assigned a maternity rotation so that I could be prepared in a manner akin to that of most nurses in the country. I was denied because of my gender. I questioned that because all of the obstetricians were men and policemen and taxicab drivers were being trained to handle emergency deliveries. 'That's different,' they said. I tried to persuade them that a male nurse would be more helpful in a delivery than a policeman, but they were steadfast in their decision. They said that if I was ever seen anywhere near the delivery room, I would be dismissed immediately.

Christman was incensed at the refusal: 'Here they were, letting these men into the delivery room when they wouldn't let male nurses in.' This difficulty was not confined to American nursing; male nurses in Canada had a similar problem. In spite of the fact that contact between female patients and male physicians was entirely acceptable, Canadian men nurses also had to learn obstetric theory without the benefit of clinical experience.

The only thing Christman could do was to assiduously study for his examination using medical textbooks. He was the first person to complete the exam paper and the woman monitor smiled when she accepted the paper and thinking he did not know the answers, said kindly: 'Don't worry—the next exam will be in six months.' As it turned out, he scored 98 per cent.

Patently, a man's motives in undertaking nursing were viewed as questionable, in some circumstances even perverted. Men could be nurses as long as they only wanted to nurse men, and, as far as Craig was concerned, provided they did not appear to be homosexuals.

Discrimination against men was also evident in the nursing literature around that time. One article in the 1920s noted that men who were employed as private duty nurses in hospitals 'could not take their meals with women nurses, interns or orderlies, so they either ate in an obscure corner of the hospital or outside'.[9] Few nursing schools in general hospitals admitted men. Even when they did, a surgeon, Willard Parker, doubted their value. He thought that male nurses, even if they were of the best quality, could not meet the demands of the sick. In his opinion men did not have the instinct for it and it was their nature to be awkward and untidy. Since he was a surgeon, presumably he did not include himself in this generalization.

Others, writing in a slightly more positive although grudging vein, thought that male nurses could make a valuable contribution to the treatment of mental illness by being role models as well as giving therapeutic care—provided they were given adequate training. Male nurses were reluctantly seen as preferable to untrained attendants in men's wards who were principally employed to protect men's modesty—and presumably women's virtue. One description of the duties untrained attendants undertook included giving enemas, colonic irrigations, rectal feedings, taking and recording temperatures, passing catheters, irrigating bladders, giving baths, attending operations and doing dressings—in other words, all the activities that nurses spent years of training to undertake. So it was no wonder that trained women nurses preferred trained men to the employment of 'educated' male attendants.

It is quite common for prejudice against a group to be overcome where a particular individual is concerned. The same director of nursing for the general hospital, Helen McClelland, who had refused to let Christman near the labor ward, later became one of his staunchest advocates. After he had worked as a registered nurse in the hospital, she wrote a reference for him couched in these terms:

> ... Mr. Christman was very adaptable, cooperative and willing to take on suggestions. He is very intelligent; no question of integrity or loyalty. His technical skill is excellent.[10]

Christman was fortunate that the teachers who led the school he attended were men with high ideals and vision. In spite of his idiosyncrasies, Craig was revered as a nurse and teacher, and his values were taken on board. In the Maltesan, published in honor of the Founders of the School by Christman's graduating class of 1939, the students said this about Craig:

> A man among men. The school stands as a veritable monument to his shrewd leadership and unswerving purpose of view. His well-planned guidance and unerring judgment have helped us over our rough, formative years. His high ideals and impeccable standards act as an ever-present stimulus to greater achievement.[11]

Both Craig and Kenneth Crummer (head of nursing education) believed that men could make a significant contribution to nursing and conveyed this to their students. Many years later Christman acknowledged the influence of Craig in particular:

... He was a marvelous person and provided me with some very early long range insights—especially the strivings that led me to the big battle to get men nurses commissioned in the Army Nursing Corps. ... Craig had spent a great deal of his life trying to establish the principle that it didn't matter whether you were a man or a woman—people out there needed nursing care, ... He was the model of a New England Puritan—a taciturn, reserved person—but his integrity and his idealism was as great as anyone's.[12]

In turn, Craig obviously believed Christman was a capable nurse. In his senior year he asked Christman to act as head nurse on the men's disturbed unit while the incumbent was on extended sick leave. Craig conveyed his confidence in Christman's abilities in a reference sent to the Michigan State Association Professional Counseling and Placement Service which presumably some one else typed for the Association's records. It is dated 29 November 1952:

Luther Christman was a student in the Pennsylvania Hospital School of Nursing for men from 1936 to 1939. He was employed as assistant head nurse, supervisor, and did private duty at the hospital. He was always well groomed. His physical health was excellent. Mr. Christman was stable and well poised. He rates high in intelligence and character [sic]. He is rated excellent in physical health, technical skill, teaching ability, leadership ability and professional interest. He was a good student and has a good record. Mr. Christman's employment record had been discussed with him, and I would be willing to re-employ him.[13]

His fellow students at the school obviously agreed with this assessment. In the Maltesan (1939) a photograph of each graduating student was followed by a brief description of their attributes written by their classmates:

> The Adonis of the class—this temperamental Pennsylvanian Dutchman has many sincere interests in life, the least of which are not nursing and military science [sic]. Being idealistic, his rugged individualism makes him stand out as destined to be both enterprising and successful.

His classmates' assessment of his potential was shrewd. But how did Christman's early commitment to nursing come about? It certainly wasn't present when he started his training when, as he said, his prime motivation was to have a job. When he was asked why he did not leave nursing when he found out how male nurses were regarded. With a wry smile, he again said 'I needed a job'.

Although his relationship with Craig was a supportive one that continued for a number of years after he graduated, it was not the real source of his commitment. Even with the virtue of hindsight, he cannot point to one defining moment or incident. But very early on he realized that he would make a worthwhile contribution if he could improve the standard of nursing care.

Today, the term patient-centered care is invoked so often it has become a nursing shibboleth. But at the time Christman's training took place, nursing work was determined more by the administrative needs of the hospital, than the needs of the patients. Even as a student, he realized that care could and should be more patient-centered:

I arrived at the view that nursing had to be more patient oriented while I was still a nursing student. I saw the difference in patient care in the wards that were heavily staffed with male RNs. In psychiatric nursing the intense one-to-one relationship was so important at that time. For some reason I had good clinical skills even at that early stage—some doctors commented on this. Relatives said that they had never seen patients behave so well as when I was looking after them. I would take the adolescent patients out into the huge grounds where there was a baseball diamond and tennis courts. I would get them playing with each other, I wouldn't even be involved, just watching. My supervisors said: "You can't do that—you are more than 300 feet away from the patient and you should always be within at least six feet so that you can control them." I got fed up with the idea that the patients have to do what we wanted them to do rather than the other way around. We had to meet the patient's needs. I became really resentful of the way patients were at the bottom of the heap—this occurred during the first year of my training.

At Christman's graduation in 1939, he told his teachers that hospital schools were not the way to educate nurses. He thought that there was too much routine and rigidity in the training with the organization of the hospital calling the tune. Christman said nurses should have a university level education just like the medical profession—an idea he promoted throughout the rest of his nursing career.

Once Christman had graduated another important event was in the offing. Christman's romance with Dorothy had continued throughout the three years of their training and once they were both registered nurses and earning money, they married. Their marriage service was held at the home of Christman's cousins, Lillian and Harry Long, in Pennsylvania. It was a small affair attended by a few of Dorothy's classmates. Reverend Bair, traveled from Summit Hill to marry them, pleased that the plans he had helped the pair to initiate had come to pass.

Near the end of his training Christman had started looking for a job. He applied for a night supervisor's position that entailed working twelve-hour shifts. He was on the verge of being appointed when he asked how long it would be before he could change to day shift. The response was 'Never, we will not allow our patients to know we have a male nurse on the staff.' Needless to say Christman did not take the job.

After a period of private nursing, he took a job as a postal clerk where he remained until WW2. Postal clerks were then paid $1800 year—much more than any hospital job would bring in. Dorothy was working 12 hours per day at a hospital where she earned 45 dollars per month, although that included accommodation and laundry. The other alternative was private nursing in people's homes. There he could earn more in a week than Dorothy had earned in a year, but it would have meant working seven 12-hour days each week. Moreover, private nursing work could be intermittent. The post office job offered consistent employment and the hours were shorter than those at the hospital. A shorter working week was more compatible with family life and left more time for further study. In any case, the postal clerk's salary was quite a comfortable income in those days, when bread cost 10c a loaf, hamburger meat was 15c per pound, coffee 15c a can and transport was very cheap.

True to his view that nurses should have a university education, Christman applied to enter a baccalaureate program. Duquesne

University was close to the apartment in which he and Dorothy were living, so he applied to enter the nursing program there. The admissions officer looked over his transcripts from high school and hospital and took him to see the dean of nursing. She refused to interview Christman, despite protests from the admissions officer. Christman overheard their conversation. The dean was quite open about her reason–men should never be allowed to gain degrees in nursing. Christman subsequently studied a few business subjects but the war intervened and any further qualifications had to wait until hostilities ended.

After WW2 he worked at the Pennsylvania Hospital for six months and did some private duty nursing. At the same time he again applied to enter another nursing degree program. The next refusal came from the University of Pennsylvania. The faculty member conducting his interview said 'If you present these credentials to our admissions office you will be accepted immediately.' The lecturer spoke with great candor when she went on: 'I know what grades you will get if you do nursing here. You will get an 'A' in all of your courses outside nursing and an 'F' in every nursing course because you are a man.' The lecturer reiterated that the nursing faculty did not believe that men should get degrees in nursing. Christman responded to this by saying he did not agree with this view. At which point the lecturer said 'Why don't you apply to some kind of field where you could use your intelligence instead of wasting it on nursing?' At that time it was commonly held that only men who were unfit for any other occupation went into nursing. No doubt the findings of the 1948 Brown Report would not have impressed the nursing faculty at Pennsylvania. The Report recommended ways of improving nursing and nurse education. One of its recommendations was that in order to ensure adequate supplies of nurses for the future large numbers of men and minority groups should be recruited!

Faced with this second knockback, Christman decided to return to his previous job as a postal clerk. Because of his family responsibilities (there were now two children, Gary and Judith Anne), his choice of universities was now limited to those close to where he was living. His next application was to Temple University and since the courses he applied for did not have anything to do with nursing, he was readily accepted. By 1948, he a university educated nurse with a Bachelor of Science degree majoring in education, fulfilling for himself at least part of what he advocated for others in the profession. The years at Temple passed without incident or any sign of discrimination, and the Adviser of the Department of Nursing Education, Temple University had this to say:

> Luther P. Christman was a student at the above university from September 1946 to June 1952. His major field of study was General Education and Psychology. He received a BS degree in Education in 1948. ... Mr. Christman was a good student. He entered into the activities of the Nursing Education Club and was a valuable member of the group. **Although I know nothing of his ability in the field of nursing,** I would suppose, judging from his work at the university, that he will be an asset to any institution with which he is affiliated.[14]
> [Emphasis added]

The discrimination that Christman faced during this period of his career provides an interesting insight into the nursing profession during that period. Not allowing male nurses to attend births when there was no embargo on male obstetricians suggested that medical training somehow enabled doctors to act professionally when attending women. By implication this diminished the professional status of nurse training. Clearly this discrimination was partly due to the widely held social views that prescribed certain roles to each gender. Yet it was also due to fears that men might take over leadership in the nursing profession. Such fears were in evidence when Christman applied to enter degree courses and when he wanted to enter the Army Nursing Corps. Despite the gender barriers put in his path, Christman became an able nursing administrator in the mental health field and gained higher degrees in psychology, both of which eventually led to senior appointments.

Mt Jefferson 'Switch Back' railway

LeRoy Craig, young Luther's teacher & mentor
Pennsylvania Hospital School for Men

Young Luther in a baseball team
(2nd R front)

'Underclassman'
Luther Christman
Maltesan 1939

'Probies'
Luther Christman
Maltesan 1939

'Alumni'
Luther Christman
Maltesan 1939

'Seniors'
Luther Christman
Maltesan 1939

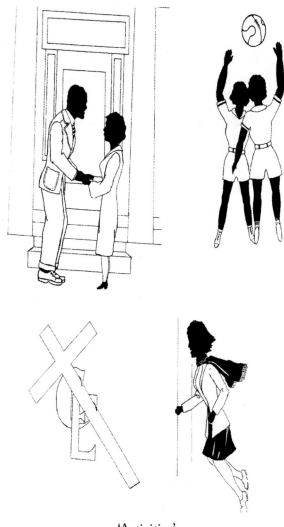

'Activities'
Luther Christman
Maltesan 1939

CHAPTER FOUR

MENTAL HEALTH AND OTHER ARENAS

It was during the middle period of Christman's career that his ability to manage organizational change firmly established his reputation as an administrator in the mental health field and he became
known as an innovator and strategic thinker. As his career developed
he became the Director of Nursing, Yankton State Hospital, South
Dakota (1953–1956). Next, the Governor of Michigan appointed
him consultant (with line authority) to the Michigan Department
of Mental Health to overhaul the mental health system in the State
(1956–1963).

For Christman personally, it was a time of further intellectual as
well as professional development. He enrolled in a master of education course and then completed doctoral studies. His postgraduate work informed his nursing administration and education work
and the reverse was also true. As an administrator he observed that
the changes he made to the structure and systems of care delivery
had substantial psychological and behavioral effects. An observation

which, together with his doctoral studies, later influenced the way he restructured clinical practice in other institutions. During this period he became active in state nursing organizations and worked to improve nurse's salaries.

Christman's first opportunity to prove his administrative capabilities came about during an appointment as an instructor at Cooper Hospital School of Nursing, Camden, New Jersey (1948-1953) where he taught anatomy, physiology, pathology, and urology. It so happened that, at about the time of his appointment, the administration of hospitals was undergoing changes. This was due, in part, to the period of considerable affluence experienced in the US following WW2 leading to a great number of hospitals being built, particularly in rural areas. Health care had become a big business. Previously directors of nursing managed hospitals, but all the building activity had led to a shortage of nurses with sufficient business experience and qualifications for these positions. Hospital administrators with education in business administration were being brought in; some of these were new graduates with little knowledge of patient care. While their business background may have benefited large institutions, it led to difficulties in small hospitals because, after a year or two, ambitious young administrators moved to larger institutions without ever having developed any deep knowledge about patient care. By contrast directors of nursing often stayed for years, and as mature experienced women, they resented young administrators calling the tune.

Fortunately for Christman, the Hospital Administrator at Cooper wanted to improve the hospital's performance and nursing care, so he asked Christman to work on a nurse productivity and effectiveness project in addition to his teaching load. Here was an opportunity to change the way in which nursing work and administrative support was structured in a hospital and Christman seized it with alacrity.

As he became acquainted with the way the Cooper hospital was organized, he realized that much of the Registered Nurse's (RN's) time was spent doing tasks which drew them away from clinical practice which was, in his view, their professional raison d'être. Answering the phone, delivering messages from one location to another, or collecting supplies from various units such as the laundry and the pharmacy, were all examples of non-clinical duties. Some of the RNs complained about the time they spent on these tasks so he decided to reorganize the system so that RNs could spend more time with patients. Such a project reflected the conclusion he had reached during his training nine years previously, namely, that care should be patient-centered rather than being organized to satisfy the needs of the nurses or the hospital administration.

The Hospital Administrator listened to Christman's views on non-clinical duties and his plan to employ ward clerks to undertake these duties. Ward clerks were not unheard of—they were first employed in the 1930s. Practically no training was required to do such a job and in Christman's view it was better to employ ward clerks than nurse aides. At that time nurse aides were expensive to employ since, because of the lack of promotional opportunities, they tended to have a very high turnover rate. The plan that Christman devised was certainly novel: it hinged on putting forward a very persuasive argument to some of the wealthy well-educated women belonging to the hospital fundraising committee. He asked them to volunteer to form a roster to work on the wards answering the phone and running messages. The women would (he hoped) demonstrate how a RN's time could be freed up if she (or he) did not have to run messages or answer the phone. Since this was a pilot program involving no cost to the hospital the Hospital Administrator readily agreed to it. The pilot demonstration was successful and ward clerks were subsequently employed at Cooper.

Some nurses fought the idea of ward clerks tooth and nail: they maintained that answering the phone kept them informed of what was going on. Christman's response was rhetorical: 'Do you really need to know there is a visitor for Mr Brown, or flowers have been delivered to Mrs Jones? Isn't it more important that you do clinical assessments?'

The next plank in his elimination of non-nursing duties was the reorganization of the ward-supply system. Nurses were always running around getting supplies—clearly an inefficient use of the best-trained personnel. At Christman's suggestion the central supply station was expanded to include a greater store of supplies and a continuous carrier service around the hospital was organized. At regular intervals the service picked up and delivered supplies including messages and memos. This caused some resentment among the RNs, since running around served another entirely different function—nurses got away from the wards for short periods and had a chance to chat with other people. When an angry deputation of head nurses came to see him, another problem emerged. Their complaint boiled down to the fact that all they had left to do was the care of the patients! Given his strong views on the centrality of patient care, Christman had little sympathy for such a complaint.

Despite these slight hitches the organizational changes were effected and Christman was satisfied that: 'Nurses were being catered to by the system, instead of nurses catering to the system'. He says that while making these changes at Cooper he learnt an important message about participatory management: 'I had gained insight into how doggedly nurses resist change. No matter where I worked after that, I always involved the whole staff in decision making'.[15]

Christman's next appointment was the first where he had the power and authority to make quite significant changes and the influence of his postgraduate education became more evident in this stage of his career. He became the director of nursing at Yankton Hospital (1953-1956).

Christman had explored various organizational theories and advocated a blend of the approaches in vogue in 1960s and 1970s.[16] Yet, Christman's strategic thinking and tactics has much in common with that of Peter Senge, a systems analyst writing in the 1990s about the 'learning organization' and ways of breaking cycles of entrenched beliefs and behaviors by finding points of leverage.[17] Christman used points of leverage in his campaign to have men included in the Army Nurse Corps and he used them again when he reformed nursing at Yankton and other mental health institutions.

In the 1950s and 1960s most mental hospital patients were in long-term care in living conditions that would be considered appalling by today's standards. When Christman arrived at Yankton Hospital he found a stark contrast between the splendid seventeen hundred acres of grounds and the ninety buildings of the large hospital complex in which the sixteen hundred residents lived. The buildings were painted a uniform color and the interiors were a gloomy brown and white. He noticed that there were bars on all the windows and that the physical restraint of patients was common. Not only that, he thought both the food and the sanitation were abysmal. Supervision was so poor that Christman discovered some patients wandering around the grounds stark naked.

Christman swiftly realized that many of the deficits in the living conditions could be easily changed. First he persuaded the painting contractor to use a variety of colors internally. In order to calm patients down, he installed a speaker system to play classical music he personally selected and graduated so that the pieces became more serene as the day progressed. The segregation of the sexes was the next issue he addressed. Two large buildings housed the geriatric patients, one each for males and females. He recruited a man to head up the women's unit and a noticeable improvement in women's personal hygiene and grooming occurred. Following that, Christman reorganized meal times so that women and men ate together. They immediately became less sloppy, fewer refused their food, and most became better behaved. Ostensibly the improvements were aimed at patients' personal habits, but they raised the patient's own pride at a deeper level. Then Christman started mixed sex geriatric wards with men at one end and women at the other. They were permitted to go for walks in the grounds together. He says: 'One nurse was all upset—"don't you know what they are doing and what will happen?" I said yes, and at the age of seventy or seventy-five, who is going to object?'

These changes quite dramatically improved the geriatric unit—it became much more sociable and orderly. Looking back on this period, Christman makes the point that mental health nursing is more than psychological therapeutic interventions. Although the ultimate effects were psychological—the changes he made were actually structural and environmental.

During the second year Christman was at Yankton Hospital, the pharmaceutical company Smith, Kline and French released a new drug, chlorpromazine, an antipsychotic agent. The drug enabled patients to become more quickly involved in psychological therapy leading to earlier discharge from hospital. The company put forward a proposal to conduct a trial of chlorpromazine to the medical administrator and Christman. The protocol included working out a range of effective dosages and monitoring any side effects. The relationship with this company was to prove very useful to Christman. The company's management was so impressed with the conduct of the trials that later on it funded his research on the efficacy of employing clinical specialist nurses.

The advent of antipsychotic agents enabled patient care to change, since more emphasis could be placed on therapy and less on custodial care. Always the strategist, Christman used two public displays to indicate that a new attitude to patient care in mental health institutions had arrived.[iii] Inviting the hospital staff to a seminar in the grounds he asked them to bring examples of their favorite restraint devices. In a spectacular public statement, the restraints were burnt in front of the staff and the members of the local press. Next the bars on the windows of the residential buildings were cut in another well-publicized ceremony.

At about this time a problem arose with the preparation of students. As Yankton was the only hospital where student nurses could have psychiatric experience, students from programs all over South Dakota received their preparation there. The Catholic orders involved in nursing education in South Dakota were concerned that Freud's theories were being included in their students' psychiatric program. The concern had come to a head because at that time the Pope had issued a statement urging all Catholics to reject the use of Freudian concepts. Worried, the nuns publicly called for Christman's instant dismissal on the grounds that he was incompetent and ruining their students' education. Although by this time Christman had some experience in dealing with controversy, this incident had the potential to publicly damage his reputation and seriously effect his career.

---

iii. Dr Edward Cowles, who was responsible for opening the first training school of nurses within a hospital for the insane in 1882, was probably the first to remove bars from windows as part of a program for turning asylums into medical institutions providing nursing care instead of being purely custodial agencies (Church, 1987:109).

The controversy had created such a storm that a statewide meeting was called. The biggest auditorium in the state was filled—latecomers had to stand. The nun who was the main protagonist knew that Christman was present. She stated that he was incompetent and a bad influence on her students because he taught Freudian concepts. His response was that all major behavioral science theorists were covered in the course and, since Freud was one of these, of course his theories were included. Fortunately for Christman, the nun's rebuttal was so ridiculous it completely diffused the situation. With amazing naiveté, the nun replied, 'I can prove his bad effects. When our students have one semester with Luther Christman they ask more questions than we can answer!' A hush fell, and then laughter filled the room—inadvertent humor had saved the day.

A nun who was head of another Catholic order rose, saying she would like to make a comment. Christman says she had a commanding presence: 'she was very tall and wore a large conical hat, which made her appear even taller'. He has vivid memories of the story she told the gathering:

> My sister [her sibling] was a patient in Yankton Hospital for eight years without showing any improvement. When Luther Christman came to head the program he chose to have my sister as a personal patient. In a few months she had recovered and was discharged. She is doing so well that not one member of my family believes she will ever have to be hospitalized again. Any man that can do this cannot be bad or incompetent.

As the nun sat down she received a round of applause. Since all the fire had gone out of the proceedings, the audience stood up and started to leave the auditorium. Needless to say, the original bone of contention, the Yankton nursing school's curriculum, remained unchanged.

There is a sequel to this story that occurred when Christman was at Rush University and his reputation as a leader was securely established. As Christman recounts it, his satisfaction that his reputation had been redeemed among his Catholic colleagues is clearly apparent:

> About twenty-five years later, I was preparing to leave my office in Chicago to give the commencement speech at the University of South Dakota, when I received a call from a nun who was now head of the Order which had previously accused me of incompetence. She said the man who was to give the commencement speech at her school of nursing had canceled due to a serious illness in his family. Since her school's commencement ceremony was the day after the University of South Dakota one, she asked me if I would be his replacement. I replied I didn't have time to write a second speech, nor could I easily change my other arrangements, which included already booked airline flights. The nun replied 'Everyone knows you're a great speaker, so we will charter a private plane to fly you back in time to meet your other commitments.' The audience was much larger than I expected with many priests attending. I inquired about the nun who had been my accuser and was told she was too ill to attend.

Subsequently Christman faced another difficult incident which was not of his making, although his position meant he had some responsibility in the matter. It occurred just as he was about to leave Yankton to take up another position. This time the potential for ignominy was averted by strong support from his staff.

Towards the end of his time at Yankton, public concern had been expressed about the behavior of staff at the hospital and an inquiry to look into these allegations was set up. The whole matter received considerable attention in the local media. The inquiry found little fault with staff behavior and that most difficulties had arisen because of inadequate administration by Dr Charles Yohe, the medical director. Staff testifying at the hearing clearly indicated support for Christman's leadership and clinical ability and the changes he had made at the hospital.[18] His credibility was further enhanced when it became known that the Governor of Michigan State had recruited him to institute his progressive mental health reforms in that state.

Now a consultant to the Michigan Department of Mental Health (1963- 1967), Christman was able to make other innovations. The introduction of fostered living care was one of them. Now that therapies included antipsychotic drugs, many long-term patients could be discharged. But these patients needed time to adjust to living away from the structured and controlled institutional environment. They needed to be monitored and supported by mental health professionals and fostered living care answered these needs.

During this middle period of his career Christman worked to raise nurses' salaries. To his mind poor pay was a major contribution to the recurrent waves of nurse shortages that beset the hospital system. Low wages also contributed to low morale and a lack of professional commitment among nurses. He was twice involved in negotiations on pay—one while he was at Cooper Hospital and the other when he was Associate Professor of Psychiatric Nursing, University of Michigan.

The background to the first negotiation was this. A survey by the US Department of Labor titled *The Economic Status of Registered Professional Nurses 1946–47* had demonstrated that nurses worked longer hours and were paid lower salaries than most workers in industry or in comparable occupational groups. In the 1950's the average hospital RN was earning $175 per month; that is $2100 per annum at around the time when the annual salary of a postal clerk was $3200-$3650 (twice Christman's salary in that position at the end of WW2). Although national nursing organizations had authorized state associations to be bargaining agents for their membership, this strategy ran into difficulties because of the Labor/Management Relations Act of 1947. The Act excluded nonprofit hospitals from the obligation of collective bargaining, so nonprofit hospital administrators could refuse to negotiate with nurses. In addition, the American Nurses' Association was strongly against strike action. Although the California Nurses' Association broke ranks by endorsing such militant action in 1966, it was another two years before the American Nurses' Association withdrew its no-strike policy.[19] So, up to the late 1960s, ordinary nurses in non-profit hospitals lacked any kind of leverage as far as salaries were concerned.

In the 1950s Christman was a member of the economic security committee for the New Jersey State Nurses Association. He teamed up with another nurse member, Alice Clarke—he says they were both 'young and eager'. The issue the committee was addressing was the low salary for registered nurses. No doubt influenced by experience with his Army Nurse Corps campaign, Christman and Clarke decided to raise public opinion about the matter. They prevailed on the press to publish articles about the nurses' poor salaries.

For financial reasons the hospital administrators in New Jersey were absolutely against raising nurses' salaries. Christman looked around for a point of leverage he could use. He and Clarke approached a group of private nurses and ask them to raise their fees by $1.50 per day. Somewhat reluctantly, the private nurses agreed. Although the increase appears marginal today, it was sufficient to be effective and nurses left the hospitals in droves to work as private nurses where they could receive more money.

The hospital administrators called Christman and Clarke in and threatened legal action to stop this move. But Christman pointed out that the fees were a private contract between a nurse and a patient, just as those between doctors and their patients were; therefore it was not a matter over which administrators could exert any control. Outwitted, the administrators had to raise the hospital nurses' salaries to retain their staff with the result that nurses gradually drifted back to hospital nursing. A couple of years later similar moves were repeated with the same result. New Jersey nurses had been among the lowest paid in the nation, but due to Christman and Clarke's strategy they became close to being the highest paid. Christman's ability to negotiate obviously impressed the hospital administrators. He was offered an administrative post in any New Jersey hospital he chose, but by this time he was fully committed to a nursing career.

In the 1960's Christman became involved in another campaign to raise salaries aimed at ameliorating the nursing shortage. At this time he was a research associate in the Bureau of Hospital Administration at the university and very active in the National League of Nurses and President of the Michigan Nurses' Association. As part of his activities as President, Christman convened a meeting of the two important stakeholders—the Michigan Nurses' Association and the Michigan Hospital Association. The object was to discuss the nursing shortage and the economic status of nurses in that state.

The background to the shortage of nurses at this time was one of hospital expansion combined with changed workforce demographics and hospital treatment patterns. First, as already mentioned, there had been expansion of the number of hospitals during the previous ten years. It was a laudable government effort to make health care more available, particularly in country areas; the result was more hospital beds but insufficient nurses to care for the patients. Second, the characteristics of the female labor force changed after WW2 partly because the number of women aged 18 to 19 years declined. This was due to a lower birth rate during the Depression. In addition, postwar marriage rates among young women between the ages of 19 and 24 years had increased. As these women bore children they dropped out of the nursing workforce until their families grew up, if indeed they returned at all. In some hospitals the nursing staff turnover was as much as 66 per cent, mainly due to the high marriage rates but also because job mobility increases when there are labor force shortages. Various retention measures were tried. Some hospitals even opened children's nurseries to attract nurses with young families back to hospital work, but the high cost of these prohibited most from providing this incentive.[20]

The third factor influencing the shortage was that hospital usage had increased. The use of antibiotics meant that many people who would have previously died of acute infections at home were being admitted to hospital for treatment and there was also an increase in the number of births in hospitals instead of the home. The implementation of hospital insurance plans in the US had also added to the number of patients admitted to hospitals. All these social changes occurred when nursing workforce participation was very low.

Hospital administrators thought that training more nurse aides and practical nurses was a quick solution—ignoring the fact that these people would be drawn from more or less the same segment of the available pool of young women. This was certainly not a good solution as far as Christman was concerned. He thought that poorly qualified nurses tended to diminish standards of clinical care and were costly if all the factors were taken into account, such as education, recruitment, supervision time and attrition rates. He maintained that money would be better spent on raising salaries in order to bring the most qualified nurses back into practice. This view was backed by a report commissioned by the Surgeon General's office.

In 1961 the Surgeon General's Consultation Group on Nursing had identified the major problems in nursing. Although the main focus of the Report was on education and recruitment, the fifth problem identified in the summary pointed to the economic status of nurses as a retention problem. 'In 1962, for example, the average nurse in a non-federal hospital earned $3,600 a year compared to the average factory worker's $4,730 and the average classroom teacher's $5,217'.[21]

Whatever problems underlay the nursing shortage in the State of Michigan in 1963, one point was clear, nurses were definitely not staying in the profession. The number of nurses actually practicing was only one third of the eligible number.[iv] In Christman's view, the prime factor for the lack of retention was low wages.

The meeting between members of the Michigan Nurses' Association and the Michigan Hospital Association (which he chaired) seemed to be going nowhere. During the long discussion bladders became full and the hospital administrators went to the men's room. When Christman joined them there, an animated conversation was going on. Since all the hospitals in Michigan were paying the same salaries, Christman saw a point of leverage. After listening for a while, he said:

> If salaries are not increased by 10%, I am calling a press
> conference to accuse the hospital administrators of this
> State of being responsible for the nursing shortage.

iv. By contrast, in the March 2000 National Sample Survey of Registered Nurses (NSSRN) it is was estimated that nearly 82% of registered nurses were employed.

There is little or no difference between salaries from hospital to hospital. I am going to accuse you folks of restraint of trade.[22]

Fortuitously, restraint of trade was receiving much attention in the press at that time. Although an argument ensued, Christman stuck to his guns and the threat worked. Back in the meeting, the requested 10% increase was agreed to. Christman suggested that the outcome measure should be the number of nurses returning to active practice. Offering to measure outcomes was an excellent strategy but, where there are a number of uncontrollable and possibly confounding factors, it can be risky, and this move could have backfired. Fortunately it was successful—over the next three years the number of active nurses in Michigan increased from 14,000 to 21,000—that is by 50 per cent.[23]

The middle years of Christman's career strengthened his conviction that he could make a difference to nursing. While his work on changing nurse salaries gave him a higher profile in state nursing organizations, Christman's contribution to the mental health field cemented his reputation as an agent for administrative change. There is no doubt that his work in changing the philosophy of care away from the traditional custodial emphasis to that of therapeutic treatment for mental illness met the challenges of those times. His work had mainly consisted of structural and environmental changes for patients and organizing nurse's work so they could give more patient-centered care. In one sense the changes he made were relatively minor, yet in retrospect, Christman sees that these changes cemented his conviction that finding ways to improve clinical competence was essential.

CHAPTER FIVE

THE ENTRY LEVEL DEBATE

A s his professional life matured, Christman began reflecting on the constituents of leadership, drawing on his knowledge of the behavioral and social sciences. He wrote several papers on the subject. In one of his papers he pointed out that defining leadership in terms of personal characteristics is an oversimplification. It is best defined in organizational behavior terms as acts of influence that have organizational relevance which goes beyond the routine. Power to act must reside in good interpersonal relationships with followers as well as being due to the knowledge and ability of the leader. Those who perceive how an organization interacts with the larger society can be highly influential in assisting an organization to achieve its ends and continuously focus on new goals and objectives.[24] If this was the agenda that Christman was setting for himself, it was a tall order indeed.

As Christman rose to positions where he could make a difference the ingredients of his own leadership style became increasingly apparent. Although not all his ideas and plans came to fruition, Christman's ability to focus on new goals and objectives, think strategically and find points of leverage often came to his rescue. But there was one argument he failed to win—the entry-level debate.

Christman has always been a vocal advocate of a single baccalaureate entry level for registration as a nurse. Indeed his first public announcement on this issue was at his own graduation in 1939 (Chapter Three). He was certainly not a lone voice in this debate. Beginning in the 1960s the American Nurses' Association (ANA) supported baccalaureate education as the entry level.[25] But he stands out as a campaigner who cogently and voraciously argued his case across a span of more than a quarter of a century. Although raising the entry level to a university degree is not a battle he (or anyone else) has won, he was enough of a maverick to keep trying. It became a running thread through the 417 papers he delivered, the 88 articles he published, and the work he did in education—particularly during his years at Yankton and Vanderbilt universities and later at Rush University. Although now retired and 88 years old, he is still doing so—but to no avail.

In 21st century America there are still three levels of nurse education that can lead to registration to practice. As other commentors have noted, the inability to differentiate levels of nursing practice responsibilities on the basis of educational preparation or any other abstract standard has proved to be one of the most intractable problems of nursing in the USA.[26]

Originally state registration agencies were set up in the days when most qualified nurses worked as private duty nurses. The registries were the central sources through which physicians, hospitals and the public could obtain the services of private duty nurses.[27] In those days it was not registered nurses that provided most of the nursing care in hospitals—it was the students who were undergoing training. Later, through the functions of the National League of Nursing, state registration boards set examinations which nurses were required to pass in order to be licensed to practice. State registration is still the only portal of entry to practice. The point of contention is not the examination and registration process itself. The debate is about the fact that three levels of preparatory education can lead to registration.

In the US, prospective nurses can still enroll in one of the few three-year hospital programs offered and gain a diploma. Alternatively they can study at a college for two years and complete an associate degree or enter a four-year baccalaureate program in a university and take out a Bachelor of Science degree. All three forms of preparation allow them to sit the state registration examinations. Of course those with postgraduate nursing qualifications at masters or doctorate level may also sit the examinations, but very few enter with that level of education. Needless to say the variability of entry preparation has not only been a hotly debated issue in the US, other countries have also faced this issue but with quite different results.

The multiple entry levels for American Registered Nurses will come as a surprise to younger nurses in Australia and New Zealand. In Australia all nursing education had been transferred to universities by 1993. From that time a bachelor degree has been the single entry requirement for state registration.[28] [29] A 'grandmother' clause allowed those nurses who graduated from hospital schools to remain on their state register. However, many nurses subsequently upgraded their qualifications to degree status. New Zealand nursing education followed a similar path and since 1996 a bachelor degree from either a polytechnic or university has been the minimum entry level. In both countries these education changes were preceded by debates of similar intensity to those in the USA.

In the United Kingdom the debate has been just as vigorous, but the outcome somewhat different. 'At present the majority of students qualify at university diploma level after a three-year, full time course that leads to registration in one of four branches: "Adult", "Mental Health", "Child", or "Learning Disabilities".[30] Recently the Royal College of Nursing recommended three-year degree courses for all nurses, but obviously there is still some way to go before a single registration applies to all.

At first glance the case for a single baccalaureate entry seems simple and persuasive. It hinges on two observations. Three entry-levels for the one profession is confusing and divisive. Parity with other health professionals is essential if nurses are to have influence in health care. Nevertheless, the reasons for the debate continuing are quite complex. They reflect the vested interests of educators, nursing organizations, state registration boards and hospitals, and of course, the vast numbers of Registered Nurses who do not have university qualifications.

The debate actually began around 1900. Concern about the variation in nurse education among hospital schools was expressed in the first issue of the *American Journal of Nursing* which included a short item that said in part:

> The diploma now held by a nurse from Smith's Corners or Split Rock Hospital, with four beds, seven nurses, and six months training, has as much legal value as that of a graduate of Bellevue, Philadelphia, or Johns Hopkins, who has spent two or three years in hard work to obtain it.[31]

In 1923 the Goldmark Report suggested that nursing education should be removed from hospitals, established in universities, and that programs should include the fundamental sciences and liberal arts, as well as professional training. These recommendations were virtually ignored and the same fate befell the findings of the mid-century studies that followed. In 1948 for example, Elsbeth Lucille Brown published a book titled *Nursing for the Future*. In a preamble to an article by Brown 17 years later, it was claimed that this widely read book had 'rent nursing asunder'.[32]

In the 1965 article, Brown, a consultant on the psychosocial aspects of patient care at Yale University, reiterated that it was her analysis of socio-economic changes and the explosion of knowledge in the physical and biological and medical sciences that underlay her views on nursing education. She pointed out that these changes meant that nurses needed more advanced preparation for their clinical roles, greater understanding of psychology and culture differences, plus a greater emphasis on teaching and research. Since these views were still cogent in 1965, Brown again stated that this learning should take place in the higher education sector.

In the 1960s and 1970s, most of the arguments for maintaining more than one level of preparation were pragmatic. The principle reason for maintaining hospital schools and diploma level education was that these programs allowed young women to enter nursing who would not qualify for entrance to colleges and universities. Another advantage was that hospital schools were close to student's homes, friends and family and attractive to those who like working in a community with which they are familiar. Diploma programs therefore recruited from a parochial pool of applicants. Workforce shortages made this argument attractive in the 1960s and mid 1970's when more than 600 hospital schools existed.

Christman saw no advantage whatever in the preservation of hospital schools. The factors that others favored in their arguments for the retention of hospital schools were the very ones he saw as disadvantageous. His views are expressed in a joint paper with Kirkman that was first published in 1972 and reprinted in 1978:

> Nurses, for the most part, have been prepared in small, single-purpose schools. These have generally been of a community or neighborhood type. The students are habitually recruited from the same local population year after year. Consequently much inbreeding took place. The unorthodox, questioning student frequently was viewed as a troublemaker and was often encouraged to leave. The removal of this student further tended to dilute the innovative potential of the system. ... Nursing education had a lockstep-like appearance as each student had the same experiences, under the same conditions, and in the same manner as all other students. ... With almost everyone in the nursing profession trained in such a fashion, it is no wonder that nurses graduated with such highly similar perceptions of nursing practice that there was little or no stimulus present to nurture creativity.[33]

Of course Christman was not the only one to be critical of hospital schools. Another commentator pointed out that originally schools of nursing became integrated with the hospital system for utilitarian purposes—the students provided a cheap source of local labor. In fact earlier on students were required to add to a hospital's revenue by caring for patients in their homes, as well as working long hours and performing menial tasks.[34]

Christman thought the schools kept nursing students isolated from students studying in other disciplines, and, as far as intellectual development was concerned, they were barren deserts compared to university campuses. Moreover, the qualifications of hospital schoolteachers were lower than those required by universities. Associate diploma and hospital school programs both had difficulty in attracting faculty with higher qualifications. Even in baccalaureate programs where faculty was expected to have a doctorate, there were insufficient nurses qualified at this level and in the 1960s and 1970s many had only master's qualifications.

To Christman's way of thinking, hospital schools became a captive of the populations from which they recruited and in turn hospitals became captive to the nurses since they depended on their own graduates for staff. Such interdependence was a major barrier to innovation and change. Further, it bred a climate that contributed to the low wages, which in turn lowered nurses' status relative to other professions. The hospitals had considerable power over the nurses; they determined 'how the nurse will practice, the tools **she** must work with, and the amount she is paid' [emphasis added].[35] As state organizations and campaigners such a Christman fought to raise salaries, it weakened the hospital's power over pay levels and this became less of an issue.

Instead of promoting a sense of belonging to a profession, Christman said the neighborhood schools caused nurses to be divided into parochial groups. Not only that, the military and religious origins of nursing were perpetuated in hospital schools. There nursing was identified with self-sacrifice, unquestioning obedience, repressive discipline and authoritarian control. He was not alone in this view. Other commentators pointed out that nursing schools maintained distinctly Victorian overtones of obedience and sacrifice, which when combined with a military-like structure encouraged conformity.[36] Moreover hospital schools emphasized skill achievement and the importance of following hospital routines. Never one to mince matters, Christman held that, in hospital schools, learning to follow set routines was confused with knowledge. This fostered anti-intellectualism and a reluctance to become fully prepared professionals.

To some extent the emphasis on rules and routines is understandable. When patients are admitted in considerable psychological and physical distress, activities and therapies need to begin immediately. In addition litigation fears tend to spread a 'bureaucratic umbrella' over the actions surrounding patient care. 'Good rule carrier outers' and 'tried and true' methods are over-valued in this situation'.[37] In Christman's view, the net effect is that patients are cared for according to rules rather than according to the clinical symptoms they present. Not everyone shared this view; one dean of medicine, pointed out to Christman that both doctors and nurses had to learn to accommodate the needs of the hospital as an institution, rather than the other way around.[38]

In any event market forces were gradually phasing out hospital schools because funding reimbursements had changed. With the advent of third party payers, such as insurance companies and the federal government, the cost of nurse education could no longer be a charge on patient care and services. When the high cost of hospital education programs became insupportable, Christman dryly remarked, 'The ideology of hospital administrators and faculties of the diploma schools went out the window as soon as they couldn't get third-party support to finance them'.[39]

The year of 1965 appears to be something of a watershed in the entry debate. The American Nurses' Association (ANA) was, and still is, a major organizational voice for RNs—in 1965 ANA membership numbered 169,000, approximately one third of the 550,000 currently practicing nurses.[40] Brown's article was only one of several that appeared in the American Journal of Nursing (AJN) that year and the articles appeared to be a lead-up to a position paper by the ANA.

The ANA position paper added additional fuel to the division and conflict. The position expressed was that nursing education should take place in the mainstream institutions of higher education. Under the heading of 'Implications' the paper acknowledged that the majority of nurses then in practice were hospital program graduates, but pointed out that economic and social factors were moving nursing towards the higher education sector. These statements flagged the demise of hospital schools to RNs, although, as already discussed, this had already begun due to financial reasons.

Not surprisingly, many RNs believed the value of their preparation was diminished by the proposed change. They argued that, since university graduates were not trained in hospital programs, they were not 'real bedside nurses'. A flurry of negative letters to the AJN followed. The following are two examples:

> Nursing education is promoting the idea that to be 'anybody' in nursing, you must have a degree, or two, in addition to our license. Students in the system believe the faster they get away from bedside nursing, the higher up the ladder they have climbed. The glory is attending the desk, not the sick. Bedside nursing is left to the aide—who under-trained and with too much responsibility—leaves. A waste of quality nursing personnel—promoted right out of the profession.[41]

> I am sure college educated nurses are necessary too, but we can't all sit at the desk. Someone has to be at the bedside.[42]

As the letters to AJN illustrate, nurses with degrees are not considered 'real' nurses'. In turn most colleges and universities did not recognize hospital qualifications as academic credentials.[43] Antagonism and resistance to single entry was inevitable, while the hospital schools failed to provide education on which further education could be easily built, and the higher education sector rejected the qualification the schools offered.

Since the membership of the ANA was virtually all hospital program graduates (as indeed were the AJN editors and most educators at that time) any suggested move to university education must have been a threat to the subscription base on which the organization depended. To Christman the ANA was a very conservative organization, where the leaders were more often intent upon getting re-elected, or getting elected, than they were on bringing about change.[44]

Nevertheless, regardless of threats to membership numbers, the ANA House of Delegates was intent in bringing about change. A resolution was passed that set a time frame for baccalaureate entry. But among other items in the resolution, it still supported two levels of entry to practice, a baccalaureate education or an associate degree. No doubt the ANA hoped to placate some of its most vehement critics by this weakened position. In any event, the resolution was largely ignored.[45]

Meanwhile the National League for Nursing (NLN) joined the ranks of supporters. The NLN is also a large nursing organization and, since 1952, the national accrediting body for education programs. In 1965, the Board of Governors approved Resolution #5 (as it became known) which supported 'the orderly movement of nursing education into institutions of higher learning'. Although the NLN came out solidly in favor of baccalaureate entry for professional practice, like the ANA, it too was under pressure from the vocal opposition from its large contingent of members who were diplomates or educators in diploma programs. Therefore, in 1965 it established two departments, one for diploma and one for associate degree programs. Nevertheless, in 1967 Resolution #5 prevailed, although it contained an explanatory statement 'stressing the need for the continuation of basic programs'.[46]

Around the time the ANA voiced support and not long after Brown's article, a series of well-funded studies of the nursing profession began. The first started in 1966, the second in 1970 and the third in 1977. The findings are in three reports by Lysaught: *An Abstract for Action (1970);*[47] *From Abstract into Action (1973);*[48] and, *Action in the Affirmation: Toward an Unambiguous Profession (1981).*[49] Christman was on the advisory board for the studies, and according to Lysaught, he made a significant contribution. The final study concluded that while some progress had been made in improving education, it was unfortunate that three entry levels to registration remained. Ironically, the ambiguity implied by title of Lysaught's third study is still there, 24 years later.

Given the money and effort that has been spent on studying this contentious issue, why is it still unresolved? One part of the answer is the composition of the nursing workforce. In 1958, approximately 86 percent of graduating nurses did so from hospital diploma programs. In 1960 and 1967 the percentages were around 84 and 72, respectively. Even in 1980 nearly one fifth of nurses were from hospital schools. Although the proportion of those with baccalaureate degrees has substantially increased since then, the workforce is still predominantly composed of the two groups with lesser qualifications. This has been governed by economics to some extent. With rising health care costs, a nurse with 'the lower, cheaper level of RN preparation (specifically, the associate degree) is going to be chosen for practice unless the nursing profession can demonstrate how the three RN levels differ in practice'.[50] Since all nurses sit for the same registration examination this is difficult to do.

In the last 20 years a great change has taken place. In 2000 the percentage of graduating diploma nurses in the US diminished to a mere seven percent. Approximately 66 percent were graduating from associate degree programs and those graduating from baccalaureate programs represented about 33 per cent. The upshot of this bitter controversy is that by 2002 associate degree programs were attracting the bulk of students, baccalaureate programs far less and hospital programs had diminished to a handful. In 2002, graduates from all three programs could still become licensed nurses if they passed state registration examinations—the USA (like Australia) has no national licensing body. Despite the ANA and NLN's attempts to institute change, a single entry at baccalaureate level appears as far away as ever.

As far as RNs were concerned the debate still seems stuck on invidious comparisons between groups with different education levels. In the papers he published and the addresses he gave, Christman attempted to move the debate into a wider context. In a 1979 paper, he drew attention to the following broader issues. First, the expansion of scientific knowledge and technology required more advanced preparation and a stronger scientific educational base similar to that of other health professionals. Second, the status of the profession would be raised if nursing achieved qualification parity with other health professions. He pointed out that dietitians, physical therapists, occupational therapists and medical record librarians all insisted on a baccalaureate for entry. Even physicians' assistants required a bachelor degree. Nurses, he said, seemed content to remain at the bottom of the totem pole and this widening education gap needed to be corrected. If nurses remained the poorest in educational background, they could not expect to have 'much influence on the form and direction of health care delivery'. Although nurses often protested that they were disadvantaged because most were women with family responsibilities and little time to study, Christman said that this was a delusion: women make up most of the allied professionals and they found the time and the means to gain university level qualifications. Furthermore:

> A worrisome prediction under these conditions is that the nursing profession may fail to attract its share of bright minds and, thus, be doomed to mediocrity. ... Nurses with less than university education are far removed from linkages with new knowledge and probably are being taught obsolescent knowledge throughout their basic preparation. Thus, they graduate with a significantly weak and questionable science base. This lack of a front line fundamental science base serves as a major structural barrier to the invention of new and imaginative patterns of care delivery systems and probably is one of the reasons why nurses cling so tenaciously to the past and resist change so doggedly.[51]

Although the paper quoted above was couched in well considered language, it is easy to see why Christman has been labeled a controversial figure. In any event, even those who shared his stand on entry levels were likely to be irritated by other reasons he put forward for nursing's lack of professional development.

The structure for nursing promotion in hospitals exacerbated the lack of professional development. As pressure to staff hospitals developed immediately post WW2, nursing could have gone either of two ways—it could have concentrated on clinical nursing and relinquished all non-clinical duties to others, but instead it went down the managerial route and left clinical duties to those with less training in nursing. Promotion patterns then ensured that most clinical care would be performed by the less educated. The hard facts were that 'the quality of care can be no better than the clinical training of the practitioner delivering the direct care to patients'.[52] Christman is fond of pointing to the rubric that no one can use knowledge they do not have.

Christman's position on baccalaureate entry was supported by his own research findings. In a study Christman conducted on organizational effectiveness in four community general hospitals, he found that errors of omission in care had a one-to-one ratio with level of preparation.[53] Nurses without degrees made the most errors, baccalaureate nurses made far fewer while those with graduate preparation made the least. This finding is important, since a patient's illnesses can be prolonged by errors of omission.

Of course, some of Christman's criticisms were met in the 1970s and 1980s by the change to primary nursing in many hospitals. In primary nursing each patient is assigned a primary RN who was responsible for his or her care 24 hours a day. But when a renewed staffing shortage arose in 2001, hospital administrators searching for more pairs of hands were forced to hire unlicensed aides who had no education in health care and only minimal training.

The entry debate still goes on and thus a key part of Christman's mission remains unfulfilled. His considerable personal charm, his clinical experience and qualifications and his research were not sufficient to win this argument. Entry level is a federal, state and organizational issue. Such a deep structural change needed strong leadership in both national nursing organizations. But, as well as having a way with words, Christman is a man of action. He proceeded to demonstrate the effectiveness of the changes to clinical practice that he espoused, first at Vanderbilt Hospital and University and later on at Rush University and Medical Center.

CHAPTER SIX

ADVANCING NURSING PRACTICE

Nursing was not discovered as a complete product, but rather was constructed by a multitude of persons, multiple settings, and within more than one context.[54]

During the middle years of his career Christman turned his attention to student education and welfare. The next story concerns a relatively minor issue but it was one that had some symbolic significance. One of the traditions he tackled was nursing uniforms. He actually addressed this issue after he had left the mental health arena and was appointed to the joint positions of Professor of Nursing and Dean at Vanderbilt University and Director of Nursing at Vanderbilt University Hospital (1967-1972). One of the first things he did at Vanderbilt was to meet with all the students and suggest they discard the traditional uniforms they wore during their training. He said that throughout the history of nursing the old-fashioned caps and aprons had stereotyped the profession. Caps were definitely out from then on. Getting rid of the rest of the traditional uniform was more difficult. Members of the school faculty who were concerned about breaches of modesty defended it. At this time female fashion decreed short skirts. Lecturers pointed out that traditional uniforms were modest, they were worn ankle length and, when students bent over, did not expose thighs or (heaven forbid) any other parts of the lower body.

Christman says his policy was never to argue with people where tradition was concerned. Instead he liked to draw on research data or use a common sense demonstration. So he contacted uniform suppliers and organized a fashion parade. The model tested each uniform style by standing with her back to the audience and bending over! Since tops and pants obviously did not expose anything at all, the faculty caved in. According to Christman, the students were so delighted they started wearing the new uniforms as soon as they could.

In order to set the context in which Christman's next contribution took place, a short digression is necessary. Nurses educated in the last 25 years would hardly recognize nursing as it was practiced and taught until the 1960s (even later in some hospitals). As noted in the debate on entry levels, much training in nursing 'was rule-based, and activity-oriented and relied heavily on the repetition of skills and procedures rather than an integration of science theory into a decision-making or planning of care'.[55] Training reflected the way in which clinical care was organized.

The task-orientation referred to above was also called functional nursing. In this model of practice, nurses were allocated certain tasks for which they were responsible—such as handing out the medications or in charge of bathing. In functional nursing the emphasis is on the task instead of the patient. It was becoming plain in the 1960s that care organized on functional lines was no longer adequate for a number of reasons. Patient profiles and the illnesses for which

91

they were admitted were rapidly changing. The discovery and use of antibiotics meant that more patients were living long enough to develop multiple chronic and acute conditions. Medical treatments now included major surgery for cancer and patients were given more complicated and diverse medications. When working in the relatively new critical care units nurses needed to be able to identify life-threatening conditions and respond immediately when necessary. Team nursing, where a group of nurses were allocated a group of patients, was one response to these new demands.

Team nursing entailed a vertical division of labor. Depending on the levels of the staff in a unit— under the supervision of a registered nurse (RN), nurse aides or licensed practical nurses would be allocated most of the hands-on work for a group of patients. Team nursing did overcome some disadvantages of functional nursing; it lessened the fragmentation of care and appeared more individualized as far as the patients were concerned.

Christman's research showed that the team-nursing model had some weaknesses. More errors of omission occurred when less educated team members were giving hands-on patient care. The RN's clinical abilities were not fully utilized and diluted by the need to manage those who did most of the nursing care. In Christman's view, team nursing did not have the level of accountability professional nursing required. Since the ultimate responsibility for care belonged to the team leader, the less educated team members tended to concentrate on putting in eight hours work, rather than concentrating on care outcomes. Whereas Christman thought that every hands-on nurse should be clinically competent enough to be accountable for the care they gave. Thus neither functional nor team nursing entailed the kind of high level patient-centered individualized care that Christman envisaged. Never hesitant about voicing strong views, Christman said that 'if someone were commissioned to devise the worst possible system of patient care, the team/functional approach would surely be the result'.[56] 'Despite the anger this may arouse in others, that is the way I look at it—team nursing has no accountability at all, and little order, if any'.[57] Not only that, Christman found that the team nursing system was distrusted by physicians.

Christman recounts how he studied four non-teaching hospitals and combed through about 1,200 records and found every patient had the same orders—vital signs were to be taken every four hours. When questioned individually, the physicians maintained that the orders were there because they wanted to ensure that a nurse would look at their patients every four hours. They said the orders needed to be there in black and white, because every day a patient would have a new nurse, depending on the team structure for that day.[58] Other commentators thought that team nursing led to patient confusion. One, Shirley Fondiller, pointed out that in team nursing 'the American public cannot differentiate professional nurses from other personnel, and patients often complained that they never saw a nurse'.[59]

As Christman had already noted in the mental health system, nurses often took on non-nursing duties because of poor hospital organization, or a paucity of funds, or both. In the 1960s, a director of nursing, described the situation in an acute hospital:

> Our nurses are spinning themselves into a frenzy here, trying to do things that ought to be done mechanically or by somebody else. Believe it or not, until about six months ago all incoming telephone calls for patients went to the head nurse's station, and she or someone else had to take messages or go down to the patient's room and tell him [or her] to ask the operator for the call—if it was all right for him to have one. ... A little

money spent on supplies and equipment would, in the long run, save a lot spent on nursing time. [It is] a system of administering nursing which hasn't changed for 25 years.[60]

Of course, Christman was not the only leader to recognize the need for change and propose a system for more individualized high levels of care. Hildegard Peplau (psychiatric nursing) and Virginia Henderson (one of the joint authors of the widely read *Principles of Nursing Practice*) are two others who were very influential. Around the same time, others were experimenting with ideas to raise the level of expertise—Dorothy Smith, for one example, arranged for a specialist nurse to act as an on-call 24-hour consultant for a unit.[61] Many other examples could be cited from the 1960s on—but these have been explored in other texts and the focus here is on the contributions of Luther Christman.

If the nursing practice changes Christman tackled mid career were to be adopted by the profession, they needed the collaboration of national and state organizations, rank and file nurses, hospitals and universities, just as the entry-level issue did. The actions of a single protagonist are unlikely to cause wholesale changes in such a large, diverse and conservative profession as nursing—no matter how determined, persuasive or dedicated the advocate happens to be. This did not stop Christman from demonstrating the effectiveness of the changes he sought in the hospitals and university schools of nursing in which he worked.

Christman's actions were often as influential as his words, sometimes much more so. Although in conversation Christman often remarks retrospectively that what he did was 'easy'. In reality, as his story continues we will see that many achievements involved going against very entrenched beliefs and interests. The actions he took to advance clinical nursing, specialist nurse education, and the nurse practitioner role now take center stage.

In a nutshell, Christman's vision for the improvement of nursing has three primary components. One, the minimum entry level for registration should be a nursing science degree (yet to be realized). Two, the most highly educated and clinically skilled nurses, working in an equal partnership with physicians, should have the authority and responsibility to perform nursing care tailored to the needs of individual patients. Three, all nursing education should be towards those ends and taught by faculty engaged in clinical practice as well as teaching and research. Christman was, and still is, fearless in his condemnation of anything less.

When Christman was first employed as Director of Nursing at Yankton Hospital (1953-1956), he found that hospital attendants did most of the hands-on nursing in the men's wards. This was the practice in most psychiatric institutions of that era. In order to implement the nurse/physician teams he planned, he devised a strategy that resulted in all care being delivered by nurses. This model was to become known as primary nursing care. Christman certainly did not use that term himself for reasons that will become clear as this part of his story unfolds.

The hospital attendants at Yankton were deeply entrenched in their positions. Christman's strategy (as far as the hospital attendants were concerned) was a return to the confrontational style he had previously found so effective when faced with intransigence concerning wages increases. This particular strategy was even more confrontational and quite unlike those he used later on to manage change in other arenas.

First, he sent questionnaires to all hospital attendants asking them to list the places and shifts they preferred and those they least preferred. Second, once the data had been analyzed, Christman reorganized the rosters so that the hospital attendants were working on the wards and the shifts they least preferred.

As he anticipated, some of the hospital attendants stormed into his office tossed their keys on his desk and said they were resigning. Christman explained he had another commitment and asked them to wait for half an hour. While out of his office he arranged with the personnel department to have final paychecks for the men ready. When he returned Christman told them their resignations were accepted and they could collect their paychecks on their way out.

During the resulting confusion the nursing staff, backed by the physicians, were able to move in and take over all patient care. Nurses were now accountable for all the nursing care, just as the medical staff was accountable for theirs. The nurses took on caseloads working in collaboration with a physician. This enabled both disciplines to work in close partnership. Most of the nurses were in favor of the partnership and some were encouraged to study for higher degrees to further improve their career prospects. Christman called it the nurse/physician team model of care.

Christman had never felt subordinate to the medical practitioners. He says that right from his early training days he had looked on them as colleagues. No doubt his collegial attitude and the fact that he was a man talking to men helped to engender their support for the nurse/physician approach. Apart from one or two of the old-style physicians, the medical practitioners were behind the innovation and communication between physicians and nurses improved. As their working relationships improved so did the care for patients. Since physicians maintained diagnosis, medical treatment and prescribing rights, the plan could scarcely be seen as an encroachment on their practice.

Christman received encouragement from physicians from all over the country who favored nurse/physician teams he had introduced at Yankton. As a result, he conducted some workshops on the topic in South Dakota and Minnesota. At first the physicians at the workshops were impressed and expressed the hope that nurses would adopt the model of care. Unfortunately a nurse from Minnesota used the term 'primary nursing' to describe the model and this effectively dampened the physicians' enthusiasm. Primary care had always been used to designate medical care and, fearing a territorial take-over the doctors' support rapidly waned. While Christman was at Yankton the term 'primary nursing' terminology was never used—he still maintains that the term 'nurse/physician teams' is more appropriate. Interestingly, 'primary nursing' became the term taken up by the profession and is used to describe one system of nursing that is still quite prevalent.

Primary nursing is practiced in many hospitals throughout the USA, although not in quite the same collaborative way that Christman intended. Chitty, writing in 1997 describes primary nursing as a model that provides every patient with an identified registered nurse who assesses their needs and plans their care.[62] This nurse is responsible and accountable for the care given to those patients in the unit 24 hours a day, and must delegate this responsibility to another nurse if the primary nurse is not on duty. As Chitty goes on to point out, a major advantage of this system, is 'that owing to the amount of time they spend with patients, primary nurses are in a position to deal with the entire person—physical, emotional, social and spiritual.' Although Christman would not have used those precise words when introducing this model in the 1950s, Chitty's words do reflect his thinking. The development of this model of care is however actually attributed to Manthey who published *The Practice of Primary Nursing* in 1980.

Christman was determined to demonstrate how the standard of care could be improved by employing well-educated clinical nurses in leadership roles. Together with Basil Georgopoulos, he initiated a major study in 1965 while he was a research associate at the University of Michigan (1963-1967). The study, funded by the pharmaceutical company with which he had previously worked, Smith, Kline and French, was completed in 1968.

In the Clinical Nurse Specialist Study, Christman's conception of the leadership role for well-educated registered nurses was formally tested at four hospitals. It is the only controlled experimental field study that has investigated the effects of clinical leadership in large hospital settings.

The experimental design involved six 25-bed units in short-stay general teaching and research hospitals with patients 'typically requiring so-called tertiary care rather than primary care of a simpler kind'. The units were closely matched in terms of size, staffing and admissions as well as a large number of other organizational variables. A series of pretests were undertaken in all six units to provide base-line data before the study got under way. Then in three of the six units Clinical Nurse Specialists were introduced to provide expert clinical leadership. For control purposes, one of the other three units remained unchanged, and the second was modified to the extent that a new head nurse replaced the previous one (to control for any difference due to staff replacement). The third of the control units included a very experienced nurse who did not have higher qualifications and who was not a clinical specialist but had been given the title just for the purposes of the study.

As well as an experiment in effectiveness, the study was a demonstration of what the clinical nurse specialist role actually entailed and what having a nurse specialist in a ward would mean for other nurses and personnel. The findings indicated that under the leadership of the clinical nurse specialist, the three experimental units outpeformed the three control units by a wide margin in nearly all areas measured. Clinical nurse specialists produced substantial gains and improvements in nursing effectiveness and unit performance. Top administrators at the hospitals generally agreed that the experiment was successful, especially since the research found that employing clinical nurse specialists actually improved the cost-effectiveness of care and was an economical use of personnel resources. Unfortunately, at that time there were few nurses available with the required level of education and a nursing shortage made the continuation of the plan difficult to implement. Notwithstanding this problem, four years later a total of ten clinical nurse specialists were employed at the hospitals.[63]

Both Christman and Georgopoulos were extremely pleased with the outcome and proceeded to write a book about the research. Since they were both heavily involved in other work the book took a few years to write. In an aside, Christman says that publishers in the nursing field were not convinced there was a wide audience for nursing research and one by one they rejected it. Finally, the authors contacted a publisher attuned to social science research who readily accepted the manuscript. Eventually it was published in 1990—more than 20 years after the research was completed.

Like many other changes that Christman made that demonstrably provided more efficient and effective care, the clinical nurse specialist idea foundered because of the episodic nurse shortages. Other hospital administrators failed to implement the clinical nurse specialist idea because instead of trying to acquire highly qualified nurses they had to concentrate their efforts acquiring whatever extra pairs of hands they could get.

Irrespective of these demonstrations and the development of new more powerful roles by Christman and others, many nurses were still satisfied with the team-nursing model. In 1998, a nurse was asked to review a book containing a collection of Christman's papers by publishers who were considering its publication. The nurse's review was passed on to him with the name of its author removed. The letter was intensely critical of Christman's portrayal of the team nursing and the nurse/physician partnership approach he advocated:

> The grim picture he paints of nursing care in the 1960's and 1970's when it was delivered under a functional or team model was overblown. The reviewer can point to highly successful experiences in numerous institutions with team nursing that proved gratifying both to the nurses who practiced and to the patients. ... Christman was advocating a system that in reality could not work in the 1960s because of the proportionally small number of BSNs and could not work today given the nursing shortage in acute care hospitals'.[64]

It is true that in the 1960s most nurses did not have much education in the basic or applied sciences. Wide professional support for the nurse/physician model of care had to wait until later in the 20th century.[65] Even then it was difficult to find nurses with suitable education.

Christman was well aware of the lack of suitable education. He tackled the education deficit during the time he was the dean of a school of nursing at the Vanderbilt University School of Nursing (1967-1972). Since Christman's aim was to have all nurses prepared in a bachelor of applied science program, the first hurdle was to have nursing recognized as an applied science. In his view, 'the nursing process is a translation of basic science into nursing care. Everything that nurses do in clinical practice comes out of some element of basic science, either behavioral or biophysical or both'.[66]

He obtained funding for a five-year period so he could develop a new curriculum and evaluate the new program against a conventional one. The project required the conventional nursing curriculum at Vanderbilt to be restructured so that the emphasis on relationship of the natural and behavioral sciences to nursing practice was clearly articulated, Christman says:

> I got a grant from the Federal Government to implement the application of science to practice. I worked with the School of Medicine so that nursing students and medical students could take the same science subjects together; for example, anthropology, chemistry and sociology. Sociologists or chemists came into to teach the theory of their disciplines alongside nursing and medical faculty who taught the application to practice. The medical faculty and medical students responded to this quite positively and so did the nursing students by and large. The anthropologist said it was very stimulating seeing how medical and nursing students responded to using anthropology in their practice caring for patients. Some nursing faculty became upset but it was a big grant and they could do nothing about it.

In Christman's view, the medical faculty backed clinical degrees because it meant that physicians would have nurses they could talk to—that is, nurses with a background in science. Implementation of the applied science program required such a comprehensive revision of the existing curriculum that nursing faculty cooperation was essential. What followed is an example of participatory management of curriculum change that involved both students and staff.

Christman readily agreed when the nursing faculty requested a three-day conference and moratorium to gather information and views about how the undergraduate curriculum could be improved. Both faculty and students attended the discussions for the first two days and the third day was devoted to final reports and consideration of recommendations. The matters discussed were comprehensive, including all phases of learning and teaching—clinical and classroom work, assignments and instructional media were all considered. The second phase of the curriculum revision took place over the next two years. Writing in 1971, Christman described the undergraduate program:

> The usual courses [subjects] labeled medical and surgical nursing, maternal and child nursing and similar types of courses are not offered. Instead there is a core curriculum that emphasizes basic science content that is spaced equally in each of the four remaining semesters. These four courses are utilized to enable students to learn the science and art of clinical practice by drawing on the theory and content of science in specific ways. ... The students are then assisted in learning the application of this knowledge in the various clinical units of the hospital under the tutelage of clinical faculty members.'[67]

Years later his pride in the program was obvious: 'Of course the word got out that, if you are going to be a nurse, Vanderbilt was a good place to go. Vanderbilt was a private university and took students from all over the States and it became known that we skimmed the US for quality enrolments'.

It was Christman's hope that taking classes together at similar education levels would go a long way to iron out differences that existed between physicians and nurses. Physicians tended to come from families in a higher socio-economic group, whereas RNs often came from humbler backgrounds. Accordingly both groups reflected the attitudes of their class and these differences often stood in the way of open communication.

Another program Christman proposed was a graduate clinical degree to prepare RNs for a more advanced level of practice, such as that of nurse practitioner. The story of this battle really commenced in the 1950's. He first proposed a graduate clinical degree in South Dakota, but his audience was not impressed. He tried again two years later at a convention of National League for Nursing in Minnesota—again no interest was exhibited. Later on, he says, the Michigan State Mental Health authority warmed to the idea and backed a funding proposal. The year was obviously propitious, since Hildegard Peplau had just inaugurated the masters' program for psychiatric nurses at Rutgers University. Around the same time a nurse practitioner program focusing on pediatric nursing was being developed at the University of Colorado. The nurse who was head of the federal nursing grants division was also supportive and eventually Christman received 'a good sized grant'.

The development of the role of nurse practitioner was one that neatly fitted Christman's view that the most highly educated and clinically skilled nurses should have the authority and responsibility to perform all nursing care. He would agree with the way in which Fairman (2001) analyzed the authority of the medical profession and would see it equally applicable to the roles of clinical nurse specialists and nurse practitioners:

> Physicians have used the process of clinical thinking to define themselves and give coherence and validity to the medical role. Physicians' position—their power and authority—was traditionally predicated on clinical

thinking skills ... Clinical thinking is, then, more than a functional process, it is the foundation upon which physicians legitimize and define their social and professional status and authority and through which they claim ownership of the patient. ... Any physician does his own history and physical work-up [the physical assessment of the patient's condition].[68]

Having received a grant to investigate the development of the role, Christman organized a group of key people to oversee the project. As well as nurses he included the head psychiatrist at Duke University, some psychologists from Minnesota and New England, and a sociologist from Massachusetts. For the next two to three years these key people went to nursing meetings around the country seeking nurse's views on the proposed program. Every presentation was tape recorded so there would be a history of all the discussions.

A major drug company Sharp and Dome, with which Christman had previously worked during a trial of a new drug, funded a scientific journalist to record all the presentations, discussions and committee meetings. Christman wanted a lively, well-written report that would engage the interest of all nurses as well as recording the arguments for and against the graduate clinical degree.

Finally a national three-day meeting was organized to present the results of the discussions. All the key nursing people were there, including three deans from major universities plus the psychologists and sociologists and psychiatrists. Then the publication of all the proceedings came out. To Christman's intense disappointment, he found it 'drab and worthless'. The publisher was the National League for Nursing (NLN). It turned out that the NLN had fired the journalist and had assigned someone with an English major (who had not been to any of the meetings) to write the report.

As the discussions on nurse practitioners and graduate clinical preparation were taking place, a debate on another matter was in full swing. It concerned the introduction of physician assistants. Both issues involved territorial disputes by the same vested interests and there was some overlap in their content. The way in which each was played out demonstrates the conservatism of nurses during the late 1960s. The conservatism of some members of the medical profession was equally evident—they were determined not to relinquish control of any part of their practice. Christman thought the views of each group were interconnected.

At the time Christman received a nurse practitioner development grant, he was still professor of nursing and dean at Vanderbilt University (1967–1972). During this period, Duke University had started a two-year physician assistant program. The physician assistant was yet another answer to perennial nursing shortages. The program was modeled on the 'military medical corpsmen training and admitted four ex-corpsmen for the first class' according to Fairman, who goes on to say that 'women were not admitted during its early years, primarily to exclude nurses, since the nursing faculty refused to accept the new role'.[69] There was a touch of irony in this refusal, given Christman's experience of the way male nurses were treated, but he was definitely against this innovation for another reason. Physician assistants would just be another group that RNs would have to supervise taking them away from providing the expert clinical care for which they alone were sufficiently educated. Admittedly there was some slight overlap of skills with the nurse practitioner role, but physician assistants would have neither the same autonomy nor the same responsibility. Of course, physician assistants were not a threat to the medical profession, whereas nurse practitioners were. As Fairman sagely points out, the words in the two titles symbolize the intended boundaries of each role: physician assistant and nurse practitioner.[70]

When Christman received the nurse practitioner grant, the biggest opposition came from the state nursing association who claimed he was trying to make physicians out of nurses. The opposition became very apparent when the Tennessee Medical Association asked Christman to be a consultant to them on standards for medical practice and organization including cooperation between nurses and physicians. When he put forward a proposal for a nurse practitioner program to the Tennessee health care organizations, this was the response:

> The Tennessee Medical Association responded with enthusiasm to having clinically competent nurses working side by side with physicians. Unfortunately, the nursing association complained that the program would make doctors out of nurses, and they refused to support the education of nurse practitioners. Medical associations also supported nurse practitioners over physician's assistants initially, but when nurses fought practitioner programs, organized medicine established physician assistant programs instead.[71]

The conservative Tennessee nursing leaders blocked an innovation that, in the 1960s, was perhaps a few years ahead of its time. Working at the cutting edge of educational innovation, it is not surprising that now and then one of the myriad of changes Christman attempted did not succeed in being taken up in other institutions. The important point is that he did have a grant for nurse practitioner program development and went ahead with it. The masters program was designed for nurses in any field of specialty and the first three admitted were all medical nurses. While still at Vanderbilt he was instrumental in setting up a family nurse practitioner service in a rural area. The service demonstrated the worth of the role to a community poorly serviced by other health personnel.

Despite a continuing debate over who should do what in clinical practice, the nurse practitioner is now an accepted role. None of the professionals involved in its development (including Christman) could have foreseen the extent to which the role would eventually find acceptance in the USA and many other countries. Towards the end of the 20th century the shortage of doctors in 'lower-paying and power-prestige areas of practice' became more acute as the number of those in the subspecialties grew. The shortage of general practitioners was worst in rural areas or poorer suburbs at a time when the demand for services was actually increasing. Since medicine was unable solve this problem alone, the time was ripe for provision of nurse practitioner services.

Christman had advanced nursing practice by demonstrating the worth of the changes he espoused during his appointments in hospitals and universities. As Sullivan has noted, 'Many of the innovations he proposed, such as clinical degrees ... [became] commonplace with accrediting agencies and certifying bodies legitimizing such work'.[72] Other changes he made were too advanced for the times and only became commonplace when taken up by others (primary nursing) or when other social events made them necessary (the nurse practitioner role).

In the 1960s, his story includes events produced by prejudice that has a far wider and deeper social significance than that displayed against men in nursing: racial intolerance. Christman was involved in two incidents. In one of these his life was threatened. The other incident exemplifies the depth of distrust that discrimination engendered in black students and neither his personal charm nor his negotiating ability could redeem the situation.

CHAPTER SEVEN

THE INTEGRATION OF BLACKS

During the 1960s, Christman became involved in the integration of blacks and whites in the university sector. As a child and young adult, Christman did not come across racial intolerance in Summit Hill—no blacks lived in the town while Christman was there. Religious intolerance certainly was a problem and Christman had witnessed the divisive effect of religious prejudice in his hometown, where some of the Protestants (including his mother) belonged to the Ku Klux Klan. No doubt these early experiences of intolerance plus the discrimination he had suffered himself, made him particularly sympathetic to the Civil Rights Movement and to the integration of blacks and minorities groups into the nursing profession and mainstream education.

Nursing, like other professions at the time, was racially segregated and discrimination was rife. When at Yankton Hospital (1953–1956), and later at Vanderbilt University (1967–1972), Christman had two quite different experiences of racial discrimination. The first incident brought home the depth of white prejudice. The second experience displayed the extent to which blacks distrusted whites—a legacy wrought by centuries of racial discrimination.

A brief summary of the situation of racial discrimination in nursing sets the scene for the first experience. The segregation of blacks and whites extended to the sick and the nurses who attended to them. The racial segregation issues are well documented so only a few facts related to nursing are presented here. In the 1920s there were 36 separate black nursing schools compared to more than 2,000 predominantly or exclusively white institutions. Even now supervisory positions in hospitals and private agencies, and the nursing professorate are, with few exceptions, the exclusive preserve of middle-class white women. As early as 1908, black nurses formed their own association with 52 members and by 1920 that membership had risen to 500. When the Army Nursing Corps admitted black nurses in 1941, it was on a segregated basis, and with a quota. Finally in the 1950s, after a sustained battle against discrimination, black nurses were admitted to the American Nurses' Association. Following that they dissolved their own association, which turned out to be a little premature—the battle was not yet won.

During the 1960s the Civil Rights Movement in America was in full voice. At this time nurse education was still mostly segregated by race, but nursing organizations were making efforts towards integration. An editorial in the American Journal of Nursing in 1961 claimed that by then 'only one state and a few districts denied American Nurses' Association membership to Negro nurses'. As the editorial went on to admit, membership was only one step along the integration path, since expressions of prejudice still existed in the profession.

Directors of nursing schools were mostly white women who seemed indifferent, or even hostile, to their black students. A 1944 national survey of black nurses by Estelle Massey Riddell brought forth such comments as 'the instructor punished us for addressing our own Negro patients as Mr., Mrs., or Miss, even though some of these people are most-highly respected citizens of our community'. [73]

In 1964, Bigham, a black nurse said young Negroes felt deeply hurt when told: 'I'm sorry, We can't hire you. We don't hire Negroes' or 'Your qualifications are good. You have passed all the examinations, but we don't feel you would fit into our program.' She goes on to say this about discrimination and hospital practices:

> Contrary to common belief, Negroes are not interested in just mixing with others. A Negro is interested in being able to live where he wishes according to his income. He is interested in being considered on an equal basis when employment is involved—not given preference, just considered on an equal basis. He is interested in receiving the same kind of medical and nursing care that others receive when he is paying the same amount of benefits.

> In one of the largest hospitals, a Negro was placed in an isolation ward rather than in the room with a white mother or rather than transfer a white patient to put two white mothers in one semiprivate room. It would have inconvenienced the white mothers to move them. In this same hospital, I, as a student nurse, was instructed to put three antipartum patients in a labor room set up for two, even though four other labor rooms had one white patient in each, though set up for two. I refused. The ironic part of it was that all the mothers were so drugged with scopolamine that they would not have

known or cared who was in the room. I was told by the
head nurse that this was policy.[74]

Despite the enormous problems black nurses have faced, by the 1970s a number reached positions of considerable authority and fame. For example, in 1973, Elizabeth Carnegie became editor of the journal, *Nursing Research*, and published an authoritative history of black nursing titled, *The Path We Tread: Blacks in Nursing (1854–1986)*. In 1978 Nichols became the first black nurse to be elected president of the American Nurses' Association and in 1996, Professor Beverley Malone became the second one. Brigadier General Hazel Winifred Johnson became the first black women to be promoted to general and received numerous honors and Clara Adams-Ender was made chief of the Army Nursing Corps in 1987. By 1990, black nurses held 'vice-presidencies for academic affairs' in four universities.

The part that Christman played in the integration of blacks into mainstream education is very small, considering the enormous problem that racial discrimination posed to the American nation. Earlier at Cooper Hospital (1948–1953) he was in charge of recruitment and admissions. Despite opposition from alumni students and some faculty members, he had made an effort to recruit black students with only moderate success. Years later, he was invited to give a speech at a dinner for alumni; the first black student he had admitted to Cooper sought him out. She thanked him for admitting her to the program—it had been the beginning of very successful nursing career for her.

When he became a consultant on the Southern Region Education Board, his job was to advise on how best to fully integrate southern universities. He believed that integration in universities should begin with the faculty and that once this was achieved, enrollment of black students would follow. As Associate Professor at Michigan University (1963–1967) and on his assignment to overhaul the mental health system, Christman employed the first two black directors of nursing in the state mental health system and three male directors of nursing. Two held doctorates and other three had master's degrees. White women nurses with baccalaureate degrees had previously held these posts. During this period he became involved in two incidents which illustrate the difficulties that integration posed.

The first incident really brought home to Christman the depth of white prejudice. It came about because of some the changes he had made at Yankton in the early 1950's. Somehow these had come to the attention of the Pentagon. A Major flew out to meet him at Yankton to discuss a problem the army had. Six conscientious objectors had been drafted as the Korean War started and their conscientious objections were founded on strong religious beliefs. The backgrounds of the six men had been thoroughly researched and it was found that they belonged to the Mennonite faith, which in the eyes of the Army justified their objection to serving as combat soldiers. The Pentagon wanted to give these men non-combatant positions as nursing attendants but finding a place where they could be trained had proved difficult. Christman said, 'he would be happy to assist Uncle Sam in any way he could'. A plan was made for the six men to learn to work as attendants for two years at the same pay rate as privates were getting in the army—$30 per month. Since many of the patients at Yankton were war veterans, the Army's proposition seemed both reasonable and desirable.

At that time there were a number of native American Indian patients at Yankton and Christman thought the care of these patients would be improved if some of the attendants were members of the same ethnic group. So he had arranged for four Indians to be employed as attendants. Christman says that during this period South

Dakotans viewed American Indians so suspiciously that they did not allow them in town at the week-ends because that was when white women did their shopping and went to church.

It transpired that the American Indians started work as attendants on the same day the Mennonites arrived at Yankton Hospital. The news of the Indians and conscientious objectors spread throughout the local community and beyond. Immediately members of the American Legion and the Veterans of Foreign Wars demanded to meet with Christman in the town square. When he arrived there he was confronted by an angry mob. They shouted that by employing conscientious objectors he was desecrating every veteran who was getting psychiatric care! They tied his hands behind his back and produced a hangman noose. Christman shouted he wanted to say something and fortunately the pandemonium subsided for a moment while he spoke:

> I, too, am concerned about the patients, but we are unable to fill these positions and unless they are filled, all patients, including war veterans, will receive less than adequate care. Everyone makes errors, but this has been done on behalf of the patients. I will return to the hospital immediately and discharge all ten of the attendants if ten men in this crowd will immediately resign their employment and accept these positions so that veteran patients will get help.

Dead silence ensued. Then the leader shouted 'Oh, let's buy him a drink' and they all went off to the largest bar in town. During animated talk over a few drinks, an agreement was reached. The new attendants could stay. It was agreed that men from both the American Legion and the Veterans of Foreign Wars would visit the veterans regularly, bring them candy and tobacco and take them for walks and they kept this promise for the duration of Christman's stay at Yankton.

The second incident occurred when Christman became Dean of Nursing at Vanderbilt University, Tennessee (1967–1972). While there he took up the integration of blacks into mainstream health education as a faculty employment issue. Believing that the integration of faculty should be the first priority, under his auspices Vanderbilt's school of nursing was the first in that university to have black faculty members. Only highly qualified black lecturers were employed—this helped ensure they were respected by the rest of the faculty and the students and were not seen as token appointments. As he recalls, the two lecturers came from New York and were very skilled nurses with doctorates and good reputations.

Recruitment had not been easy—many nurses said they did not want to live in the South, which was having real problems with integration at that time. It was not just teaching on a predominantly white campus that was the problem for the nurses. It was all the other racial discrimination that living in the city brought with it—going to the theatres and shopping were examples of activities where racism was likely to be confronted.

During his time as Dean he contacted the new president of Fisk University, Stephen Junius Wright, with a view to attracting some blacks into nursing education programs. He already knew Wright who had been a professor of physics at Michigan University while Christman was there. Fisk, a private university for blacks, had been funded in 1865 by wealthy northerners in an effort to increase the educational opportunities of freed slaves and it had become a university in 1867. So it had a hundred-year history at the time of Christman's contact.

Christman describes how he saw the situation:

There had been a huge migration north to work in the automobile factories. Blacks could make more money in the North. Student bodies in the white universities in the South resisted integration, but in the North there was little resistance to integration at this time. When affirmative action came in, all white universities were under pressure to have a representative number of black students (35 per cent) or the government would withhold funds. In a way it was a double standard since the reverse did not apply to black schools.

At their meeting Christman and Wright agreed that any students who wanted to become nurses could transfer from Fisk to Vanderbilt once they had taken all the required sciences. So that Fisk programs would be at the same standard academically as Vanderbilt, Christman suggested the sociologists at Fisk get a grant to upgrade their sociology course. In the meantime lecturers from Vanderbilt would go to Fisk and take turns at teaching the sociology courses.

Christman taught the first sociology class at Fisk and what transpired was evidence of the deep distrust that black students felt towards whites:

> On the first day I went to start the sociology course and immediately there was uproar—they wanted to tell me what to teach—that blacks have been treated badly by whites. I said, no that was not the purpose of the course and mentioned the president's name and said we were colleagues working together. The student's response was—you are white and you don't belong on this campus.

The next sociology lecturer from Vanderbilt was escorted off the campus by a group of husky black youths. Finally the Vanderbilt faculty had to give up the faculty exchange idea—the black students were too militant. Nevertheless the integration plan was not a total failure—some black students did transfer into the Vanderbilt School of Nursing.

Although a small player in the arena of black integration into higher education, by the end of the 1960s Christman had become an acknowledged nursing leader. When Christman became director of nursing at Vanderbilt Hospital and a dean at Vanderbilt University (1967-1972), this kind of joint appointment was most unusual and placed him in a uniquely powerful position to influence the way that nursing was taught and how it was carried out in the hospital. Notably, he was the first man to be appointed a dean of a nursing faculty. However, these prestigious appointments did not put an end to the prejudice Christman had experienced as a male nurse. Instead he was subjected to an act of gender discrimination that was more public and blatant than anything he had previously experienced. As well as being a great personal disappointment, the event put a cap on one of his professional ambitions and constrained his influence as a nursing reformer. He was nominated for president of the American Nurses' Association, but was not elected. Christman had finally hit a glass ceiling.

CHAPTER EIGHT

HITTING A GLASS CEILING

By the time he reached middle age, the boy who really wanted to be an artist and only entered nursing to have a job in the Depression years, had become a nurse with an established career and considerable professional influence. According to his colleagues Christman was a man of considerable personal charm, with a quick smile and an easy manner. He is described by a nurse (who met him briefly at a conference) as a man in the prime of his life, striking in appearance, with a full head of silvery hair, a fair skin, and a trim figure.[75] One of the men who worked closely with him, Jerome Lysaught, describes him as insightful and incisive but always ready to consider alternatives, often displaying a 'pixyish' sense of humor.[76] Although many women nurses saw him as a potential threat, many others became friends and supporters—among them are Helen Mc-Cullen, Shirley Fondiller, Karen Morin and Virginia Henderson. The women he worked with were convinced he had the qualities of a leader. Although as Christman himself pointed out in one of his papers on leadership, personal characteristics are only some of the ingredients of leadership capacity.[77]

A colleague, Faith Jones, remembers him as a charismatic figure able to convince others by logical argument. She thought Christman a good listener and a straight shooter with a strong ethical outlook.[78] Another colleague, Mildred Fenske, said he has 'an unusual ability (atypical of many nurses) to work collaboratively and constructively as a colleague and/or peer'.[79] To Shirley Fondiller, Christman had 'that elusive quality of inventiveness, productivity and courage to step ahead when others hold back.'[80] Virginia Henderson, with whom he exchanged views about how nursing could be improved, often wrote congratulating him on the work he was doing. Although he inspired the confidence of many women nurses, others were still prejudiced against male nurses as the following episode graphically illustrates.

In 1968, on the second day of the annual convention of the American Nurses' Association, Luther Christman stood on a balcony observing the cocktail party in full swing below. From this vantagepoint, he could see two groups of three nurses circulating among the clusters of delegates. The Californian nurse standing beside him told him then that these two groups were spreading rumors about him. Christman had been nominated for president of the Association and the vote was to take place the following day. There was only one other candidate, Dorothy Cornelius.

On the first day of the convention, the delegates had set the criteria by which candidates would be judged. The Association wanted to raise the visibility of the organization and emphasize the scholarly side of nursing. The retiring president, Jo Eleanor Elliot was instrumental in Christman's nomination and had approached him to stand as a candidate on the basis of his scholarship, since he held baccalaureate, master's and doctorate degrees and had a high profile as a nursing academic. He had written a chapter, 'Nursing the mentally ill' in *Practical Nursing* by Broadwell and Von Gremp (1995) as well as publishing 27 articles in journals and delivering 68 papers at conferences on mental health or nursing in general. He was a consultant to the Southern Regional Educational Board, and a member of the Editorial Board for the journal *Perspectives in Psychiatric Care*.

A reputation in clinical nursing and a strong contribution to nursing organizations were other important criteria. Christman had made well known and widely acknowledged changes to clinical nursing in the mental health field. He had made a significant contribution to raising nurse's salaries. He had been president of the Michigan Nurses Association from 1961–1965, the second male president of a state association and the first to be elected for two terms. Previously, in South Dakota, he had been a vice-chairman and served on the board of that state's nursing association. He knew he had the support of state nursing organizations, 'Some 42 or 43 States nominated me.'

The delegates had expressed the desire for a president whose career showed a continuous progression. At this point Christman was the Director of Nursing at Vanderbilt Hospital as well as the Dean of Nursing at Vanderbilt University. And, as already noted, he was the first nurse to jointly hold both academic and clinical leadership positions and the first man to be appointed a dean of nursing. His credentials contrasted quite starkly with those of the only other candidate.

Dorothy Cornelius' highest qualification was a diploma and her highest position was that of assistant director in the Cleveland, Ohio blood bank where she had worked for many years. Cornelius had some experience in nursing organizations and was the executive director of the Ohio State Nurses Association at the time of the election.[81] Since she had not written a book or published in journals, her lack of academic activity combined with her career record meant she did not meet any of the stated criteria.

In the 1960s the feminist movement was extremely vocal and equal opportunity legislation was being sought, although not yet implemented in the USA. In this context it was not surprising that the election attracted much attention from the press—a man was about to be elected president of a women's profession. Both male and female reporters turned up to report the result and they told Christman they wanted to interview him as soon as the voting was over. Given that Cornelius scarcely fitted the delegates' stated criteria, Christman expected that his election was virtually a foregone conclusion and so did the journalists attending the convention—at first.

On the first day of the three-day convention the reporters told him his election was a 'shoe-in'. The journalists had already interviewed many of the nurses as they registered for the conference. They estimated 72 per cent would vote in favor of Christman. The morning following the cocktail party (the day of the voting), they said he did not stand a chance, 'you're dead, there is a whispering campaign that you are a homosexual and the delegates have turned against you'.

His supposed sexual preference was not the only baseless rumor. One of the other delegates, Gregory Johnson, gave this account of the rumors in a letter to Steven Merrill who was undertaking a

v. Permission to place the letter in the Christman archives was given by Johnson to Merrill in a letter to Christman dated 17 February 1997.

121

doctoral study of Christman's career.[v] The gist of the rumor carriers' statements made to Johnson were these:

"Dot" or "Dotty" Cornelius was a far better candidate because:

> Dr Christman was "behind" the ANA position defining the difference between "technical" and "professional" nurses [who held a Bachelor of Nursing Science degree]. Therefore he was "against" diploma nurses, and Dotty was a diploma graduate herself.

> Dr Christman's unique appointment at Vanderbilt (Dean and Director) was not an achievement of which to be proud. The appointment was either exploitation on the part of Vanderbilt, or an attempt to save money, by which Dr Christman had been duped. Or it was the front edge of an attempt to have Schools of Nursing take over nursing services. Why did Johnson think other Deans and Directors remained in separate positions?

> He was a homosexual—couldn't Johnson tell? The fact he was married didn't matter: that charming manner was a clear signal that he "swung both ways".

> A man nurse would never be president of the ANA.

The basis to Christman's supposed antipathy to diploma nurses was that earlier on Christman had supported an ANA contention that eventually all nursing education should take place in universities. Since this was one of his most strongly held views, it was expressed in many of the papers and addresses he had given during this period. Because of this contention, he was said to be against clinical nurses who held diplomas from hospital programs—at that time around 88 per cent of the workforce. None of the other points the rumor-mongers made had substance, but one certainly bit where it hurt. Once again the specter of a male take-over of a woman's profession had been raised and it hit home. The thought of a man becoming president of one of the most influential nursing associations in the USA was just too dreadful contemplate!

The election of Dorothy Cornelius as president was announced in the American Journal of Nursing (AJN) in June, together with a short commentary on the shrieks of joy from the delegates.[82] There was one final irony. In October of the same year, a letter to the AJN commented on a resolution by the American Nurses' Association. According to the writer, the ANA was opposed to discrimination on 'whatever basis—race, **sex**, creed, colour or national origin' and had resolved that 'the organization would work on all levels to alleviate this condition!'[83] [Emphasis added].

Earlier in his career, Christman (partly tongue in cheek) had listed his Laws of Behavior. Alas, the last two in particular were born out by the rumors of some of the nursing leaders and the vote:

1. Everyone wants the world to be in his/her own image.

2. No one can use knowledge they do not have.

3. In every instance, given the free choice between rationality and irrationality, everyone opts for irrationality as their first choice of behaviors and is only rational when forced to be rational.

4. Most people, under most circumstances, generally will do what is right, if they know what is right, and **if the temptation to err is not too great**. [Emphasis added]

Twelve years later during an interview with Jerome Lysaught, Christman referred to this incident as the 'Dallas Debacle'.[84] Although his defeat was primarily rested on resistance to a man becoming president of a major nursing organization, his eagerness to move nursing education into universities was obviously influential. In 1965

ANA membership numbered 169,000—only about one third of the 550,000 currently practicing nurses. Obviously any move that might alienate the RNs on whose subscriptions the organization depended was to be avoided. Another possible factor was his knowledge that the ANA was seriously in financial deficit, although this was not made public until later. Christman says that '… many members of the board of directors and staff were irritated that I had found such mismanagement, and they blamed me for finding the deficit rather than becoming concerned about the fact it was there.[85]

Whatever the complexity of factors that underlay his defeat in the election for president, he was completely out-maneuvered by the wily nursing leaders who used three points of leverage—anti-intellectualism, prejudice against homosexuals, and fear of women losing control of the profession. In constructing his own strategy, Christman had failed to fully evaluate the strength of the threats to his nomination. As he stood on the balcony watching the cocktail party, Christman had already guessed the likely outcome, but it was too late, the opportunity to counteract the work of mischief-makers had been lost.

This was not only a personal defeat, it turned out to be an impediment in some of his campaigns to advance nursing. Some of these, such as the single entry level for registration debate, hinged on winning national support from professional organizations and through those avenues, the rest of the profession. In hindsight, the bid for president of the ANA occurred too early in his career. If his nomination had occurred when he became Vice President of Nursing Affairs at Rush University (1972–1978) and his reputation in America and overseas had been established, arguably his bid for election would have been successful.

CHAPTER NINE

WOMEN'S DOMINATION OF NURSING

... nursing led the way in organizing the first real system of vocational training for women on anything like modern lines and in building the first independent associations of professional women. In all these activities they were helped by the steady advance of woman's education and the growing strength of the whole woman's movement.[86]

When Christman failed to be elected president of the American Nurses Association in 1968, it clearly demonstrated that nurses were still prejudiced against male nurses. The fear that men might become a dominant force in nursing had started much earlier in the century, although an important theme in the development of the profession, it has received little attention by historians. Because prejudice against male nurses played such an important part in Christman's career, the historical underpinnings of gender discrimination and the reasons for its continuation will be discussed in this chapter and the following one.

The topic of male gender discrimination is one that few nursing histories even mention, let alone explore in any depth. Kalisch and Kalisch are two authors that do deal with the bias men faced.[87] In *The Advance of American Nursing*, under the sub-title of 'The harassed male nurse', these two authors make the point that in both WW1 and WW2, male nursing skills went largely unused. They go on to say that barriers to their employment and education appeared to be due more to do with sentiment and tradition than any actual ineptitude based on sex. They point out that most nurses and the general public seemed to adhere to the stereotypic view 'that women alone should take care of the nursing'. Bullough and Bullough are another pair of authors that discuss the prejudice that men experienced in their book *The Emergence of Modern Nursing*.[88]

Roberts is another author who sees men's place in nursing as sufficiently important to devote a chapter on the topic.[89] Her history of men's participation in nursing covers the period from just before the turn of the 20th century to the end of the 1940s. Roberts suggests that one of the reasons for male nurses not being regarded as part of mainstream nursing is due to most being trained as psychiatric nurses whereas women were general nurses; a view that has some substance. She thinks the reason men were not admitted to membership of the American Nurses' Association (ANA) until 1930 was simply due to them being forgotten—rather than evidence of any feminist plot. Be that as it may. Later in this chapter it will be argued that the determined efforts of early leaders to keep nursing as a woman's profession appears to be linked to the early 20th century struggle for women's suffrage.

When Christman was ready to embark on his career in the 1930's he had no idea what belonging to a minority group in a female-dominated profession would mean. Nor did he realize how this might affect his subsequent career. At the time male urology or psychiatric nursing were the only fields open to men and the number of male nurses was very small, only about 0.5% of the nursing workforce. Earlier on this was not the case.

Men have been nurses since the first recorded nursing school was set up in India in around 250 AD—only males were seen as 'pure' enough to become nurses. Military, religious and lay orders of men provided nursing care throughout the Middle Ages, and the Knights Hospitaler is just one example among many. In 1808 a hospital in San Antonio only employed men but by 1908 a sign on the nursing quarters read 'Entrance to no man's land'.[90] How inadvertently prescient that sign turned out to be!

Professional men nurses have existed in the United States almost as long as female ones. Originally, there were at least four accredited schools of nursing especially for men. One was the Mills School for Male Nurses at Bellevue Hospital, New York that was established in 1888. Together with Bellevue School of Nursing it is now part of the Division of Nursing, College of Medicine, New York University. The Alexian Brothers conducted two other nursing schools, one in Chicago and the other in St. Louis. The fourth was the Pennsylvania Hospital School for Men, the one that Christman attended.

In the early 20th century men were in demand for the care of men patients admitted with fractures, heart conditions, genitourinary problems, venereal disease or alcoholism. According to one nursing history, 'personnel in psychiatric wards wonder how they ever got along without them'.[91] Since the expectation was that they only nursed men, male nurses found work in heavy industry such as mines or on construction sites. Private nursing was common in those days so they also nursed men in people's homes.

There was however, considerable ambivalence about the value of training male nurses. Well before the 20th century they had developed a reputation for drunkenness and incompetence that was hard to shake off. For example, a 1914 hospital manual weighed up the arguments as to whether male nurses were a good thing or not and appeared to decide in the negative. It stated that previously male nurses were often 'a composite of drunkenness and genius' but found them 'more virile and less finicky' than females. The manual went on to say that it doubted that men would go into nursing if they were fit for another occupation.[92] At Mills Training School for Male Nurses, male student nurses were compared to the female students at Bellevue Training School and the males were found wanting. According to Dr Abraham Jacobi, male pupils did not generally learn as fast as he had hoped. He thought the men were more interested in the patients as medical cases, but most of them were not observant of patient's personal needs and they failed to take care of the wards properly.[93]

It is not surprising that the men appeared less competent than the women at Bellevue Training School or those at the New York Hospital School. Among the students at that time were Lavinia Dock and Lillian Wald, two of the most revered early 20th century nursing leaders. Both Bellevue and New York schools had a reputation as a school for women from well-educated, middle and upper class families and attracted women from all over America and many other countries. Some of the students had previously been teachers or librarians for example. Details of the schools the women went to together with the occupations of their fathers, brothers and sisters were kept, presumably because at that time women's social status was determined by family connections. To a certain extent that also applied to men, but usually their social status was judged by their occupation. Information on the backgrounds of male students was not kept at Mills Training School, but the characteristics of the students at the Pennsylvania School in Christman's time suggest that many would have had some training in other disciplines.

The Nightingale, a nursing journal in the early part of the 20th century, predicted that men would not remain nurses for long. Interestingly Mottus' study of the graduates from Bellevue and New York schools shows that 13.6 per cent of men did go on to do medicine while only 1.4 per cent of the women did.[94]

The low regard in which male nurses were generally held in the first half of the 20th century explains why LeRoy Craig was so insistent on high standards of education and behavior at the Pennsylvania Hospital School for Men. During the time Christman trained there, the men were seen as effective nurses. Helen McClelland, the director of nursing reported to LeRoy Craig that she was surprised at how much the standard of care had improved when properly trained men nurses attended the male patients. She pointed out that their psychiatric training helped male patients adjust to their stay in hospital.[95]

Women certainly predominated in the training schools between the 19th and mid 20th centuries. When Christman started his training in 1936, there were only 68 schools that accepted both men and women, and many of these were state mental hospitals. Lack of appropriate housing facilities was cited as the main reason for schools in general hospitals not receiving men. Such excuses are reminiscent of those used for not admitting women to male-dominated fields later in the 20th century—lack of female toilet facilities was a frequent one.

The low reputation of men in the profession in general and lack of facilities were not the main reasons for discouraging men, many of whom became good clinical nurses. The discrimination Christman experienced was clearly aimed at preventing men gaining positions of power in what was perceived as a women's only profession. Such discrimination relied on beliefs about the supposedly inherent characteristics of men and women and their appropriate roles. Female nurses were not the only ones to exhibit the prejudiced attitudes that bedeviled Christman's early career—male physicians were just as stringently opposed to female doctors.

The male-dominated medical profession conveniently believed women were the weaker sex whose place was in the home and certainly not in such a prestigious profession as medicine. Physicians certainly did not fear that women would take over the leadership of medicine—such a fear was unthinkable. Instead they thought that the encroachment of women would lower the prestige of their profession. The history of the development of both professions was redolent with discriminatory practices as physicians and nurses strove to protect their interests.

Nursing was a female-dominated profession and early nursing leaders wanted to keep it that way. Traditionally, the justifications were that nursing was one of few occupations open to women, and it was seen as consonant with women's natural caring role. These attitudes were inextricably bound up with the women's issues of the day, most notably women's battle for political enfranchisement in the United States.

Writing from a feminist perspective in 1996, Lewenson describes the situation in which nurses saw themselves:

Since the late nineteenth and early twentieth centuries, the nursing profession has been labeled a predominantly women's profession.

Not only were women considered naturally suited to nursing, but the caring role itself "naturally" belonged to the women's sphere. Throughout the modern nursing movement, the caring role, practiced by nursing, has been subordinate to the curing role, practiced by physicians. Although the nursing profession offered women work in what was perceived as a woman's occupation and considerably less threatening to men, nursing nevertheless faced paternalistic control. For the most part, men feared financial, emotional, and social loss of power to the women who marched for women's rights or worked in typically male-defined occupations. Discrimination rested not in women encroaching on men's private sphere of influence, but rather in a paternalistic society wanting to control all spheres, especially women's work.[96]

Professionalization and suffrage together helped entrench the view that nursing was indeed a woman's profession and that, in a paternalistic society, it needed protection. The history of the development of the major American nursing associations was clearly linked to suffrage. Some vocal nursing leaders saw that as women they would be powerless in their professional and personal lives without it. One of these was Lavinia Lloyd Dock.

In 1886 Dock had graduated from the Bellevue training school, one of the first schools to be founded on Nightingale principles. A prolific writer, Dock compiled the first *Materia Medica for Nurses* and was the main author of the four-volume *History of Nursing (1907 and 1912)*. In 1911 she published a manual for nurses *Hygiene and Morality*. The development of public health nursing in the USA is attributed to her. A vigorous and deeply committed feminist, she led the first group of suffrage pickets to the White House in 1917. By the time she retired in 1922 she had become a leader in the suffrage movement and the strongest feminist voice in the profession.

According to Dock, nursing and the women's movement were inextricably tied together since male medical dominance was a major problem confronting the development of the profession. Although Dock saw nursing and women's issues as inseparable, this was not a view held by many other leaders of her time, let alone the rank and file. The topic of suffrage was hotly debated in various nursing state, federal and international nursing associations. Nurse leaders, like Lavinia Dock and Linna Richardson (to name only two nurses actively supporting the suffrage movement), were convinced that battles for state registration, professional status and reasonable working hours would not be won unless women were seen to be equal to men in the political arena. These leaders saw nursing as an oasis to be preserved and nurtured by women for women. In 1909 Linna Richardson expressed this reason for suffrage: 'Ours is a **women's profession** in a man's world, and we need to realize that men will take much less interest in our advancement than we take ourselves'.[97] But there was one powerful group of men who were vitally interested in curtailing nurses' influence: the doctors.

Physician's stereotypic views on how women should think posed a great threat to nurses' autonomy. A 1928 report by the Committee for Grading Schools (nursing schools) noted the professional relationship between physicians and nurses. The report said that physicians were worried that nurses might become too independent, too educated, and too theoretical, to serve as professional sub-ordinates in caring for the physician's patients. Many physicians were against shortening working hours stating as the reason: self-sacrifice was a woman's privilege! Lavinia Dock thought they were simply feathering their own nests since many owned private hospitals. Dock's response was 'I think nurses should stand together solidly and resist the dictation of the medical profession in this as in all other things'. Obviously women nurses had to fight their own battles. Yet according to Dock, nurses should be trained to be obedient: 'This obedience to orders, founded in principle and animated by an intelligent interest, is the dominant characteristic of the new system of nursing and is the secret of its success in its professional work'.[98] Such were the contradictions faced by a female profession in the society of that time.

Women doctors could have been allies in the early 20th century, but they were too busy fighting discrimination themselves. They had previously supported nurses by setting up nursing schools in hospitals for women in the 19th century. When the first wave of feminism was at its strongest in the US it had been easier for women to become doctors. Ironically, when American women gained the right to vote in the 1920s, they found acceptance into male dominated medical schools more difficult. The reasons given for excluding women from medical programs centered on stereotypic views of women's position, and supposedly innate qualities. For example, Harvard graduates saw women only in subordinate, almost menial capacities, and thought that women were incapable of reaching a professional level similar to that obtained by men. The Harvard faculty invoked a so-called 'fundamental law' to explain their exclusion: the primary function of women is to bear and raise children. The story of Alice Hamilton illustrates how these attitudes influenced their behavior to women doctors.

In 1918, Harvard hired Alice Hamilton as a medical lecturer in Industrial and Occupational Medicine. Hamilton was never promoted above assistant professor in her 15 years at the faculty. Certain employment conditions were aimed at keeping her profile low—she was not allowed to march in academic commencement processions and not allowed into the faculty club. Allowing Hamilton to be employed as long as she remained more or less invisible is reminiscent of the strategy Christman encountered when told he would only be employed if the patients were not aware there was a male nurse on the staff.

Despite the very vocal leaders on the subject of suffrage and nursing, the profession was basically conservative. Rather than becoming involved in wider social issues, the American Journal of Nursing preferred to give Florence Nightingale's views as the reason for maintaining nursing as a women's sphere of influence. An editorial early in the 20th Century stated that, according to Nightingale, 'The undivided control of nurses in all that relates to their teaching, training, and discipline must lie in the hands of women, themselves trained, and occupying positions of undisputed authority within the limits assigned to them.' The editorial went on to identify a number of problems facing nursing. One was the increasing 'male encroachment' as students in respectable nursing schools.

Beliefs about the innate characteristics of men and women kept women doctors in their place and certainly colored nurses' views on how men were to be treated in their profession. The view that every man was ambitious by nature and craved power must have worried the nursing leaders. When the American Nurses' Association (previously the Nurses Associated Alumnae—note the use of feminine noun) was formed before the turn of the 19th Century, their articles did not include men. Although this was unlikely to have been a feminist plot as Roberts has noted, it did emphasize the female domination of the profession. It was not until 1930 that men were admitted, but no special attention was given to them until the Men Nurses Section of the ANA was organized in 1940.

The views of those who were against male nurses in this and the preceding chapters were quite overtly and clearly stated. The inescapable contradictions in these views were conveniently glossed over. It is clear from Christman's own examples that men should be kept in subordinate positions regardless of their aptitude and commitment. It is understandable that women should feel possessive about what they saw as their profession at a time when career opportunities for women were few. Nevertheless it is ironic that women who, as the largest social group to suffer discrimination, should themselves become perpetrators of such blatant discrimination against a small minority.

In the 1960s and 1970s professional organizations were beginning to examine discrimination of male nurses as an issue and research on men's position in the profession began to be reported in journals. While a few changes had taken place by the latter half of the 20th century discriminatory practices against male nurses were still common.

CHAPTER TEN

20TH CENTURY DISCRIMINATION

'… male nurses have their own story, one which illuminates questions of work and gender from another angle.'[99]

Historically, gender discrimination has been seen as a woman's issue. The Historical Encyclopedia of Nursing under the title 'Gender Issues' devotes 18 pages to this topic, but all except one paragraph is about discrimination against women. [100] That single paragraph describes Christman's campaign to do away with the taboo against men in the military nurse corps. It notes that he carried the crusade for gender equity into other venues, and gives a brief outline of his career. The exclusion of men from university schools of nursing and from obstetrical nursing does not rate even a sentence. The only authors to take issue with the 'matriarchal history perspective' in nursing are Canadian and they do so in the context of their study of the 'Resistance to commissioning of men in the Canadian Military between 1952 and 1967'.[101]

Even in the 1960's gender stereotypes still appeared in the textbooks for student nurses. Men were portrayed as patients in need of care and women were portrayed as caring nurses. Faculty used feminine pronouns when discussing nurses. Even authors such as Bullough and Bullough who are among the few writers to discuss men's role in nursing at length sometimes slipped into its use. Moreover, when practitioners were almost exclusively white females, the general population naturally assumed that nursing was a white woman's profession. To most people the word 'nurse' meant white woman—except when qualified by the words Black or male. In the 21st century men in the profession still refer to themselves as male nurses.

By the early 1960's the American Nurses' Association was, to some extent, addressing discrimination against men and its effects. An American Journal of Nursing editorial titled 'Men in Nursing' suggested that, although a survey had found that 22 out of 27 other countries valued men's contribution, there was still evidence of real discrimination against men in the US, noting that many schools still did not admit them.[102] Bullough and Bullough, writing in 1969, pointed out that American 'nursing had still not demonstrated that it is an attractive proposition for the man'.[103] Nor had the profession really demonstrated that it wanted men. As Equal Rights Amendments (ERA) and other laws prohibiting sexual discrimination were progressively enacted, a few schools of nursing did do away with discrimination on the basis of gender. In the AJN, one educator noted discrimination on the basis of sex was not permitted at her school, but she went on to say that at first she had 'serious qualms' about teaching male students obstetrics. Nevertheless her fears were quelled when she found her 'pioneer' male students were interested, intelligent, willing and able to perform all midwifery care—but she stopped short of allowing men to put the baby to the breast!

Not all schools of nursing have been in favor of male students, however. The Mississippi Women's University came before the Supreme Court of the United States in the 1980s because it denied otherwise qualified men from enrolling. 'Justice O'Conner held that the practice was in violation of the equal protection clause of the Fourteenth Amendment'.[104]

In 1994, a Florida nurse, Bruce Wheatley filed a complaint against a hospital with the Equal Employment Opportunity Commission (EEOC) because he was 'denied employment in labor and delivery and postpartum care units because he was a man'. The EEOC found in his favor and in its determination said that the hospital 'acknowledges that males are not hired for positions in the birthing areas of the hospital, due to the comfort level of patients'. Therefore regardless of how qualified a male candidate is, based solely on his gender, he is still deemed ineligible. In a final ironical twist in this discriminatory tale, Wheatley eventually found work in a gynecological clinic run by women!

In the last ten years, the question of whether men are taking over leadership positions has again surfaced in nursing journals. In a review of research literature, Foreman concluded that men were indeed slightly over-represented in administration, education and some specialty areas such as critical care.[105] But two caveats must be borne in mind. Full time work is often a requirement for higher positions and the proportion of males to women who work full time is about 9:6 respectively. Moreover men are unlikely to interrupt their careers like women do in their child bearing years and advancement in any field often depends on continuity of employment, a factor that had not escaped Christman's attention (see below).

Whether over-represented in positions of power or not, the fact remains that men are still a small minority in the profession. In the

USA, between 1969-1972, the percentage of male nurses was approximately 3 per cent, in 1992 it was 4.3 per cent, and in 2000 the percentage of men had risen to 5.4; a total of about 146,902. According to a report on the National Sample Survey of Registered Nurses in 2000, the number of men is growing faster than the total RN population. On the other hand, male graduates are currently leaving the profession at twice the rate of women: 7.5 per cent of men left nursing within four years of graduation, compared to 4.1 per cent of women. In 2000 the total RN workforce was estimated to be 2,696,540 by National Sample Survey of Registered Nurses (NSSRN), so men are still a very small minority.

Discrimination against men is not just an American phenomenon. The situation is similar in other English speaking countries. British men have had similar experiences. In the UK male nurses were admitted to the main Register of Nurses following the Nurses' Act in 1949. But it was it took another ten years for men to be allowed to become members of the Royal College of Nursing. After a 1964 review of nursing, the Royal College of Nursing championed sexual equality in nursing and dropped the title "matron" as it implied the head of the nursing service was expected to be a woman. But it was not until 1983 that men were allowed to become midwives. An amendment to the 1975 Sex Discrimination Act in the UK finally made it unlawful to discriminate against men, but there are still exemptions on the grounds of decency and privacy, or where personal services are best provided by women. [106]

Nevertheless, men in the UK have taken up leadership positions in a way that would have really alarmed early American nursing leaders. By 1987, although making up fewer than 9 per cent of nurses in Britain, more than 50 per cent of men held chief nurse and director of nurse education posts.[107] The reason for men holding such a disproportionate number of high positions in the UK nursing workforce has been attributed to the Salmond Report (1966), which pro-moted a more rational managerialist structure in nursing. Thus the stereotypic view that men are best at managing worked in their favor. In Australia, although men were only five per cent of the workforce, eight per cent were already in management positions by 1985.[108] In Canada, male nurses made up 5.2 per cent of the registered nurse population in 1996—however they represented 7.9 per cent of stu-dents enrolled in nursing programs. Men are certainly over-repre-sented in high positions as shown by the Canadian 1992 survey data; 15 per cent occupied management positions although men only rep-resented about four per cent of the nursing workforce.[109]

The top jobs in nursing emphasize leadership skills, technical competence, and unconditional dedication to work—qualities typi-cally associated with men. Therefore men may choose nursing as a career because they believe their sex will be an advantage since they will be expected to be leaders, administrators and change agents.[110] Thus even at the beginning of the 21st century, the stereotypic views of men and women explored in the previous Chapter still have cur-rency. This is so, despite the investigations that show men enter nurs-ing with a desire to care for people[111] and are no different to women in this regard.[112] The desirable characteristics for nurses are those associated with the best of both genders, i.e. warmth, understanding, gentleness and independence, self confidence and decision-making capacity.[113]

Like females in male-dominated professions, male nurses have a load of stereotypic baggage with which they have to deal. But their quandary is quite different—on the one hand they are a minority in their profession, and on the other, they belong to the dominant group in the society in which they live. The profession expects them to play minor roles, while social expectations require them to lead. In 1962, the year before Christman became Associate Professor of

Nursing at Michigan University; he belonged to a very small group of males who held higher education positions. Despite being a little over five per cent of RNs, men constituted only a little over three per cent of faculty.[114] Since about two per cent of the male faculty were deans during Christman's time, the fears of early leaders were far from being realized.

Regardless of research on why males become nurses, their relative occupational status and other characteristics, there is still the unanswered question of whether an influx of male nurses would really make a difference to the profession. Christman thinks it would.

In a paper he delivered in 1970 Christman made a number of observations on how he thought more men would make a difference to the profession.[115] Stressing the disadvantages of having a predominantly female profession was unlikely to win favor among female nursing leaders, even when these are patently obvious. Some of the points he made are controversial and open to question as the following annotated summary indicates.

In this paper, Christman points out that men are more stable workforce participants, and likely to have uninterrupted careers. Men do not leave nursing to raise families or leave jobs because their spouse takes a job in another state—social stereotypes and gender characteristics work in their favor in this respect. It follows from this observation that workforce stability would have a beneficial effect on recurrent nursing shortages. Certainly recent research has found that more men stay in the profession (85 per cent) compared to women (35 per cent). *This line of argument ignores one factor. Nursing shortages tend to encourage job mobility by both men and women since other jobs are easily obtained.*

Christman goes on to point out that 97 per cent of men work full time in every field but only 32 per cent of women do. Women tend to prefer part time work, especially after they are married. If one third of the nursing workforce were male, he estimates that there would be a surplus. *No doubt this is true, but this line of reasoning ignores the fact that men are still the primary income source for families and are therefore difficult to recruit into nursing if other more highly paid occupations are available.*

Nevertheless Christman thought more male nurses would have a positive effect on salary negotiations. *Other commentators agree and point to the economic bias associated with women's work and education suggesting that more male nurses may act to redress this low valuation, therefore their presence or absence may well be a barometer of the economic value that society places on nursing.*[116]

Christman also argues that, since additional men would make the workforce more stable, this would increase the lobbying activity of the American Nurses' Association which he thinks is dampened down by the shifting population of part-time female nurses. He also makes the point that male nurses are freer to pursue postgraduate education just as their counterparts do in other professions. This freedom occurs because in many cases married men do not make the same contribution to child raising as their partners do, even though gender roles are not as highly prescribed as they were in the past. Christman firmly believes a more highly educated nursing work-force would benefit the profession and the patients for whom they care.

In another paper, Christman pointed out that:

> The overwhelming femaleness of the profession con-
> tributes to the slowness of development in regard to
> knowledge. It is not that women are less intellectual or
> less capable than men, instead, it stems from the fact
> that women, for the most part, are interested primarily

in marriage and rearing a family and only secondarily in work careers. The many disjunctions in the work life of nurses means that most do not have the opportunity to move steadily forward and to make a substantial contribution to developing new nursing knowledge.'[117]

This implies that, if there were more highly educated male nurses, then more men would occupy high positions and the research output would be greater. Certainly the UK experience suggests that this would be the case as Ryan and Porter have noted. However, the extent to which the scholarly output of male nurses in higher positions in the UK has actually contributed to professional development remains to be researched.

In the 1970 paper Christman suggested that men are more capable of dealing with physical demands now that patients need more intensive care and nursing work has become more stressful. *No evidence is given in support of this contention.*

In the belief that gender colors interactions between members of the health care professions, Christman thinks that more men would reduce tensions between nursing and physicians and administrators, since most of the latter two are male. *This contention seems to be based on his observations of 'male companionship' roles. It is a contention that would have got right up the noses of early nursing leaders and no doubt today's feminists would see it as perpetuating the 'old boys' networks which women are consistently up against.*

Having made these points, Christman acknowledges that some women have forsaken marriage and family life and all that goes with it, to make significant contributions to nursing, and that others have combined family life with very successful careers. The crux of his argument is that these women have been too few to provide the leadership necessary to take up the opportunities that would further the development of the profession. *There is no guarantee that a larger number of male nurses would benefit the profession in general, it may simply increase the supply of career-oriented people.*

Obviously the lack of male nurses is a social and cultural feature of the last 150 years in the USA. The reasons for this are many. As has been noted, masculinity is not associated with caring, which is considered a feminine quality with the result that men in nursing are often characterized as homosexual. Homophobia makes it difficult for heterosexual as well as gay men. 'The stereotype of homosexuality forms a major obstacle to many heterosexual men who might otherwise consider pursuing nursing as a career'.[118] [vi]

Economic circumstances have alternatively served as an attraction and a disincentive to men to enter nursing. There has been a tendency for more men to enroll in nursing programs during economic recessions. When economic circumstances are good, the low status and relatively low wages of nurses make the profession unattractive—men are supposed to be achievers and breadwinners. New opportunities, such as becoming a flight nurse in an emergency flying ambulance service, may attract men seeking adventure and jobs requiring a high level of clinical skill. Positions such as this require fairly long-term career planning however, which few beginning students undertake.

Even when men are attracted to nursing programs, they could still face the kind of discrimination that Christman experienced. Characteristically challenging the prevailing orthodoxy, Christman believes that affirmative action for men is the only answer:

---

vi. It is interesting that the issue of female homosexuality is not raised as a barrier for women; except in the Army Nurse Corps as Snodgrass (1999:118) has noted. Nursing manuals in 1930,1936 and 1940 did warn against intense female relationships, but did not overtly mention female homosexuality (Melosh, 1982:64:65).

I think there is only one viable alternative, and that's something women never thought would happen—traditional women's professions should be put under affirmative action, to make sure that men get represented in these fields. Women will be helpless to fight that movement, because they would look ridiculous saying that everything that women have they must hold, but everything that men have they must share.[119]

Applied to traditional male professions, affirmative action has proved very successful for women. When affirmative action came into being, the typical medical school admitted one or two women each year, whereas in 2000/1 women are 44.6 per cent of medical students nationally and they now account for 24 per cent of the total physician population. But affirmative action has never been applied to female occupations. Christman remembers an Affirmative Action group from Washington D.C. descending on Vanderbilt University to warn the faculty deans of the funding repercussions likely to ensue if the University did enforce affirmative action. They turned to Christman, dean of nursing and said 'You do not have to conform to affirmative action in any way'.[120]

The equal employment opportunity legislation does have some substance inasmuch as men cannot be kept out of employment or programs. But equal opportunity does not entail taking *any positive action to recruit men*, in the way that affirmative action requires for women. Since, in nursing, men only comprised about five per cent, Christman asks 'Can you imagine how the women in this country would be talking if medicine or dentistry only had five per cent of females working in it?'

Christman thinks that one of the first priorities is to employ male faculty. Male faculty should be both academically talented and good role models—Christman has no time for tokenism. But he found difficulty in recruiting men, despite various attempts as he rose to positions where he could influence both the recruitment of staff and the enrolment of students in nurse education. He realized that any attempt to increase the numbers was not going to be an easy task:

> The position of men in nursing is somewhat analogous to that of the black community in the open society. Much of the drive must come from the black citizens themselves if they are to attain a new status. ... It will take much hard work on the part of men in the profession to encourage large numbers of young men to consider careers in nursing as professionally exciting.[121]

Daniel Pesut, president of Sigma Theta Tau International, certainly believes men who enter nursing need commitment and courage. He remarked in an interview:

> Men who choose a career path in nursing are more likely to have engaged in soul searching about their personal and professional values and beliefs. Humans who engage in intentional soul searching often are sustained by the courage of their convictions in spite of stereotypes, minority status, voice and influence.
>
> Most male nurses I know have made a conscious philosophical commitment to the values of care and service. Male nurses embody the courage of their convictions. Nursing is a means for them to align what they believe with what they do. Male nurses make value statements every day because of who they are and what they commit themselves to do.[122]

The need to attract more men into nursing certainly concerned Christman, but was only one part of his vision for nursing. The need to promote advanced clinical skills and raise nursing's authority and visibility remained high on his agenda. Christman had three new organizations in mind. The first of which would place clinical skills at the forefront of professional expertise, while the second would raise the profile of the nursing profession in relation to other health care disciplines. The third organization would bring male nurses together so their contribution to the nursing profession would be more widely accepted and recognized.

CHAPTER ELEVEN

RAISING NURSING'S PROFILE

Christman's professional endeavors often extended beyond boundaries of his occupational appointments. Already an active member of established state-nursing organizations he became involved the founding of two new national organizations—the Academy of Nursing and the National Academies of Practice. He also worked to revitalize the existing male nursing organization.

In regard to the first two, one of his prime motivations was to raise the profile of nursing *vis-a-vis* other health disciplines. When President of the Michigan Nurses Association (1961-1965) he raised the idea of forming an American Academy of Nursing. Each state nursing association would nominate a nurse for election to the proposed academy. Christman's conception of such an academy was that it should be similar to academies in medicine and dentistry that brought practitioners together who were recognized clinical experts in their field. Naturally, since improving clinical competence was part of his overall plan for the development of nursing, he was of the view that clinical competence should be the prime criterion for election to the academy. Christman knew that clinical expertise was the basis for selection to the National Institute of Medicine (he is a member) and he used this an example. Christman says he had already worked out a way of measuring clinical competence that would serve the purpose, however he never got the chance to put it to the test. The American Academy of Nursing, after a long gestation period, ended up a somewhat different organization to the one he had originally envisaged.

In some respects the proposed criterion was ahead of its time. He proposed the academy in 1964 when there was no recognized clinical ladder of progression in hospitals, and there were few clinically based postgraduate nursing programs. Advancement in nursing was achieved by moving to administrative or educational positions—therefore nursing leaders tended to come from this background.

Christman contacted the other presidents of state organizations and received their support. He arranged for the proposal to be put on the agenda for the next American Nurses Association (ANA) convention in 1964. At this convention a plan for restructuring the ANA was put forward to the delegates. An article outlining this plan was published in the American Journal of Nursing in April. A diagram titled the 'Functions of proposed ANA specialty divisions' included the proposed academy in the structure with a note saying 'if indicated', which suggested there was prior knowledge of the academy proposal.[123]

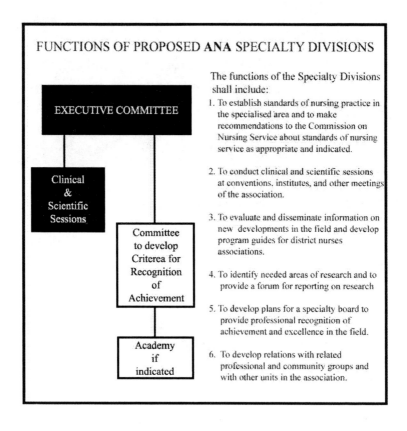

FUNCTIONS OF PROPOSED **ANA** SPECIALTY DIVISIONS

EXECUTIVE COMMITTEE

Clinical & Scientific Sessions

Committee to develop Criterea for Recognition of Achievement

Academy if indicated

The functions of the Specialty Divisions shall include:

1. To establish standards of nursing practice in the specialised area and to make recommendations to the Commission on Nursing Service about standards of nursing service as appropriate and indicated.

2. To conduct clinical and scientific sessions at conventions, institutes, and other meetings of the association.

3. To evaluate and disseminate information on new developments in the field and develop program guides for district nurses associations.

4. To identify needed areas of research and to provide a forum for reporting on research

5. To develop plans for a specialty board to provide professional recognition of achievement and excellence in the field.

6. To develop relations with related professional and community groups and with other units in the association.

In order to lobby for his proposal, Christman arrived at the convention the day before. He found the executive officer wanted to see him. She said that the officers on the board of the ANA did not want to support an academy and asked him to withdraw the proposal. Not surprisingly, Christman refused. A delegation from the board then came to his room and repeated the request. He asked their reason and the response was that the proposal over-emphasized the clinical side of nursing. Christman's response: 'Then let the House of Delegates decide the issue'.

In the meantime those opposing the Academy proposal had developed two strategies to try and delay voting. When the convention was in session, a member of the board introduced a motion to make Christman's proposal the last item on the agenda. This was an obvious ploy, since, as is the case with most conferences, many of the rank and file leave early to return to their home states. Christman says the members of the board had an additional delaying tactic up their sleeves. When the item finally came up, the president said she wanted to present the Dean of Columbia, who proceeded to make a twenty-minute speech. But, when Christman eventually presented his proposal, the majority of delegates left at the convention accepted it. A report of the convention in Nursing Outlook said:

> The House of Delegates gave the ANA Board of Directors two years to provide a plan for the establishment of an Academy of Nursing to foster the development of clinical specialization in nursing. The academy is intended to offer a means whereby **expert clinical nursing practitioners may be identified and recognized.** It will also offer clinical specialists an opportunity for discussion of scientific theories and nursing problems.[124]
> [Emphasis added]

In 1968, the American Journal of Nursing published a report of a conversation between the president of the ANA and three other office bearers. Rozella Schloetfeldt, chairman of the ANA Commission on Nursing Education, raised the issue of identifying clinical experts and recognizing them in some way such as by certification of membership of an academy. The president, Jo Eleanor Elliot, responded that the first step to identifying the members of an academy was the certification of practitioners, which entailed setting criteria and this would be completed by 1970. Schloetfeldt thought this time frame was too long. To expedite the process, she suggested their peers should identify members for the proposed academy.[125]

It took the ANA another five years to actually implement that idea. The clinical criteria for election to the Academy were dropped. Christman ruefully commented: 'The only criterion for election to the Academy became popularity'. Each state association could nominate one member to belong to the first group, although that nurse did not have to be from their own state. When the State of Maryland nominated Christman for the first group to be admitted, he was not accepted! He did become a Fellow of the Academy when he was nominated again in 1974. By this time he was well established as the Vice President of Nursing Affairs and Dean of Nursing at Rush University—what else could they do?

At his first meeting as a fellow, naturally Christman raised the topic of restoring clinical competence as the basis for selection to the Academy, but the president gagged any debate on the issue. The current criteria for selection call for outstanding contributions to the discipline and are quite wide ranging. Suggestions as to which outstanding contributions would be acceptable do include contributions to nursing practice—but actual individual clinical competence is not mentioned.[126]

It seems that some of the antipathy to his ideas that surfaced when he was nominated for president of the ANA in 1968 had surfaced again. Christman says that at this point in his career most nursing organizations and their leaders had little time for his proposals. In turn, Christman is still critical of both the American Nurses' Association (ANA) and the National League of Nursing (NLN). He thinks the ANA is 'just inching along, often when giant steps are required.' At the behest of their membership, the ANA has tried to be the 'collective bargaining arm and a professional organization at one and the same time' and Christman points out that this has not worked for other professions—teaching is one example. As far as the NLN is concerned, he thinks its stand on entry levels for practice puts it beyond the pale. The NLN still recognizes hospital school diplomas, associate diplomas of nursing and baccalaureate degrees and act as though all programs are equal, exemplified by the phrase 'A nurses is nurse is a nurse'.[127]

Another source of antagonism was his view that the lack of development of the profession was due to the predominance of women who are more family than career oriented and that more career dedicated men would redress that situation. Whatever the truth of these assertions, it is by no means certain that more men would necessarily promote the kind of development that Christman envisaged. Christman is not unsympathetic to the difficulties of studying while working and caring for a family, a job that usually falls to women. He freely acknowledges that studying while working is an enormous additional load and it is not surprising that many women are not sufficiently career oriented to study for higher degrees and develop research portfolios. Nevertheless, as Christman points out, women in other professions manage to do just that. Such views are likely to fall on deaf ears when most of the members of an organization are working women with families, so it is small wonder that leaders of nursing organizations failed to support his ideas.

Christman's ideals for the Academy remain unrealized. Nevertheless it became a robust organization. Ironically, given the opposition to his ideas, in 1995 the Academy recognized his overall contribution to the profession by deeming him a Living Legend.

Christman's idea of establishing National Academies of Practice (NAP) was modeled on another organization—the National Academy of Science. In the latter, leaders from the myriad of scientific disciplines met to communicate with each other to foster interdisciplinary work and generally promote scientific endeavors. The NAP was established in 1981 and is now an umbrella organization for national academies of ten health-related disciplines: dentistry, medicine, nursing, optometry, osteopathic medicine, pharmacy, podiatry, psychology, social work and veterinary medicine. Membership is through election as a Distinguished Practitioner or Scholar in one of the individual academies.

The idea for such an organization occurred to Christman while he was at Rush University (1972–1987). Several colleagues had the same idea. Nick Cummings, a psychologist was one. At that time Cummings was head of a foundation that was heavily endowed and responsible for one of the main hospitals on the West Coast. Cummings was very interested in clinical competence in his own discipline. Other interested people included the Dean of Nursing at Columbia University, a dentist and a social worker. Christman does not remember all the people involved but recalls that the initial group eventually numbered eight. Each one of the eight picked ten or twelve people from their disciplines they thought to be outstanding and liberal enough to want to break down barriers and encourage interdisciplinary cooperation. Gradually the ten became one hundred from each health science group.

Instead of congress being lobbied by individual pressure groups, the foundation members thought that a combined voice in matters that concerned them all would be far more effective. The NAP wanted to establish an integrated position—a broad picture of what was good for the patient and the country. As Christman looks back, he says that founding the National Academies of Practice was an uphill battle. All the major professional organizations had their own agendas framed by the particular interests of the members whose subscriptions finance them—a factor he had already encountered in nursing organizations. At first, every time the NAP lobbied congress on an issue, one of the big professional organizations would intervene with a different position and congress would back off. Christman had to ruefully admit that very few professional organizations are really interested in interdisciplinary cooperation—they are interested in promoting themselves.

Nevertheless, the NAP has conducted seven Interdisciplinary Health Policy Forums that have emphasized how the professions can work together. These have resulted in papers on health care for the elderly, plus one titled *Health Children 2000* and another titled *Ethical Guidelines for Professional Care and Services in a Managed Care Environment.*

The National Institutes of Practice requires nomination to be based on either evidence of expert practice, or scholarship, or both. In 1985, Christman's achievements were recognized by the NAP when it presented him with the Distinguished Practitioner award. Christman thinks the NAP is probably still struggling and that the interdisciplinary journal they started may be discontinued because of lack of a sufficiently wide subscription base.

The continuing discrimination experienced by male nurses was still well to the forefront of Christman's mind in the 1970s. As far as Christman was concerned, the 1968 'Dallas Debacle' had emphasized that a deep and pervasive opposition to men was still present among American women nurses. No doubt this personal experience of gender discrimination led to his interest in a third organization, the American Assembly for Men in Nursing (AAMN). The ideas behind its establishment were that there should be a forum for male nurses to deal with gender issues, and that the number of men entering the profession should be increased.

When Christman became really interested in raising the profile of male nurses an organization was already in existence—the Michigan State Assembly for Men in Nursing. To enhance its membership potential however, men were recruited from any state. About ten years after its birth Christman was invited to speak at one of its yearly conventions and says he was amazed when several hundred men turned up. Like any new organization, the Assembly had its share of controversies and it was just teetering along when the name was changed to a more inclusive title: The American Assembly for Men in Nursing. Slowly the membership increased and it now has 280 members and publishes a newsletter called Interaction, a name suggested by a colleague, Shirley Fondiller. It is a truly non-discriminatory organization. Membership is unrestricted by age, color, creed, handicap, sexual orientation, lifestyle, nationality, race, religion, or gender. Thus AAMN is open to both men and women. When its board established the Luther Christman Annual Award to recognize and honor his efforts to advance the profession, President Ford was the first recipient because of his consistent congressional efforts to raise the level of the profession.

The object of the AAMN is to provide a forum for discussion of the problems men face. A Professor of Nursing, Karen Morin, says she joined the Board in order to understand the plight of her male colleagues and students and this experience alerted her to the subtlety of much discrimination against males.[128] The goals of the Assembly are to wholeheartedly encourage men to become nurses and join together with other nurses in strengthening and humanizing health care.[129] Although unstated, these goals do imply that fighting discrimination is one of AAMN's aims. As Virginia Henderson notes in a letter to Christman in 1987:

> Men nurses as a "minority" in a "woman's profession" are indebted to you, I believe, for creating a forum in which their particular interests can be increased and the recruitment of men into the occupation promoted. All of us are grateful for your participation as well in the principal local, state, and national organizations.[130]

Christman's involvement with these three organizations had not deflected him from his main mission and his agenda was still the unification of nursing and education. Opportunities for demonstrating how this could be done came during his appointments at Vanderbilt (1967–1972) and at the Rush University and Medical Center (1972–1987).

CHAPTER TWELVE

THE RUSH MODEL OF NURSING

When Christman took up the positions of Vice-President of Nursing Affairs at Rush-Presbyterian-St. Luke's Medical Center and Dean of the College of Nursing at Rush University, the prospect of starting a school of nursing from scratch in a new university must have seemed irresistible. Now he would have a chance to fully implement the role he believed nurses should carry out. He was determined that faculty in the University and Medical Center would practice and teach in the clinical areas, lecture in the school, conduct research and act as consultants.

The president of Rush University, Dr James Campbell, was a driving force in the university's development. In 1977, Campbell described Rush's mission in these words: our chief objective is patient care with the implementation of education in a rational manner, scrupulously managed, balanced and forward looking and made vital by research'. Christman was a consultant throughout the initial stages of development and the collaborative relationship that grew between these two men would eventually permeate the whole institution. Christman's influence was obvious when Campbell asserted that nursing must be given 'the stature and responsibility which this profession must rise to under modern expectations of professional performance and compassionate care'.[131] So right from the start Christman had a unique opportunity to develop his vision for nursing.

Rush University and the Rush-Presbyterian-St. Luke's Medical Center each have an interesting history. The Center began as the coalescence of three institutions. One was the Rush Medical College, which had been founded in 1837. Following World War 2 it was decided to discontinue the College, although for years it had provided the main source of medical practitioners in the Midwest. The other two institutions were St Luke's Hospital and the Presbyterian Hospital. Each of these had started schools of nursing before the turn of the century but had formally merged in 1956.

In the 1960s the Presbyterian–St. Luke's Medical Center closed its hospital school of nursing but remained a clinical site where students from the adjacent University of Illinois could receive clinical experience. Around the same time Rush Medical College sought to re-establish its charter. Part of the plan was to merge the hospital and the medical college as a medical center and university. In 1969 the Center became the Rush-Presbyterian-St. Luke's Medical Center—given the length of the title it became known informally as 'RPSL' or simply just 'Rush'.

Both the hospital and the University are private institutions that, although conducted as businesses with boards of management, do not have shareholders. They are, using Australian terminology, 'not-for-profit' enterprises. Both are well endowed and have been the recipients of large government grants but remain primarily dependent on student and patient fees for their operation. Situated in the immediate vicinity are a veteran's hospital and the University of Illinois which also has a medical center, so although these institutions serve different sections of the local population, they are in competition for staff with Rush, if not for patients.

Christman's appointments not only included the posts of Vice President, Nursing Affairs and the Dean, College of Nursing, but also that of Professor of Sociology, College of Medicine. The multiple appointments were important both strategically and symbolically. From the outset nursing was accorded the same status as medicine and other disciplines. In an interview with Urban Health in 1980, Christman said:

> [It is a] transformation of a major urban hospital into an academic center in which nurses are obligated by their position to make major contributions to the achievement of the medical center's goals of quality care, quality education and quality research.[132]

In the period immediately prior to its reorganization as RPSL Medical Center, the hospital was similar to others in the 1960s and early 1970s. Before Christman arrived at Rush, the model for nursing care delivery, although called team nursing, was basically functional nursing and care was fragmented into various tasks allocated to members of a team. As one Rush nurse commented:

> … There was a loss of the planning aspect of the nursing process. Nurses did little more than follow physician's orders for care. While patient assessments, patient teaching, and discharge planning were probably being done, there was no organized method of documenting or evaluating such care. … Much nursing time was spent in non-nursing activities like housekeeping, transport, errands, and supplies. There were no clear lines as

to who was supposed to do a task, and the time it took to find who was supposed to do it, call that person, and then wait until someone carried out the task prompted the typical cry, 'It's easier to do it myself'.[133]

The closure of the old hospital's nursing school had exacerbated the local shortage of RNs. Therefore the staff in Licensed Practical Nurses (LPNs) and nurse aides plus medication technicians who were 'trained by the hospital, whose function was the administration and documentation of all medications'.[134] So, when Christman took up his appointments, nursing care at the hospital incorporated the very features he had sought to eradicate elsewhere. Characteristically, he wanted functional patterns and non-nursing activities eliminated and all care delivered by RNs according to the primary nursing model he had previously introduced at Yankton Hospital in the 1950s.

In 1973, after a hospital-wide committee at Rush had discussed all the 'ins and outs' of changes to the care delivery system, a pilot study of four units was set up. Although the shortage of RNs at the time meant that staffing still included LPNs, RNs became the primary nurses with responsibility for all patient care. There were no longer functional assignments to take TPRs (temperature, pulse and respiration), blood pressures etc. The primary nurse placed the nursing documentation at the patient's door, so charting could take place as it was done, rather than at the end of a shift. Other improvements in documentation were introduced. The physician order sheet now came in triplicate: one copy in the chart, one to the Laboratory Liaison Clerk for labwork and the third to the pharmacy, thus removing some of the steps that are likely to increase errors and omissions. Common progress notes were introduced which did away with the usual separate notes for each discipline. The progress notes provided a running narrative of a patient's stay construction with input from physicians, nurses, physical therapists, nutritionists and others as various treatments and outcomes occurred.

Two other inter-related changes did away with many of the non-nursing activities. One was the introduction of an area director. Area directors oversaw all non-nursing and non-medical activities like house-keeping, transportation, pharmacy and central supply. The other change was that the work of auxiliary departments was decentralized. For example, Laboratory Liaison Technicians received orders for laboratory bloodwork directly from the physician's order sheet and were responsible for drawing blood, taking it to the blood bank, giving the written results to the unit clerk. They also tracked down lab reports. Previously tracking down could have wasted up to four people's time—the unit clerk, transfusion nurse, transporter, as well as the charge nurse.

The ideal level of staffing in the pilot study took a while to achieve, but gradually nurse aides were phased out and placed in other jobs in the hospital. Nonetheless the project attracted little resistance and was deemed a success. No doubt this was due to the wide consultation process at the beginning and to support at the highest levels. Needless to say, as the Vice-President of Nursing Affairs, Christman was right behind it and so were the president, Campbell, and the Vice-President Administrative Affairs, Yvonne Munn.[135]

It was not only nursing care that needed a shake-up at Rush. The hospital's organization was heavily bureaucratic and top-down decision making was commonly practiced. Both Campbell and Christman saw this as unwieldy and ineffective. Under their combined leadership, Rush-Presbyterian-St. Luke's Medical Center was reorganized as a matrix. The aim was to have all the hospital resources integrated horizontally and vertically and more focused on patient care. Components in the matrix included managers, physicians, nurses and basic scientists. The advantage of a matrix-type organization was that it made it 'feasible for the members of each component of the organization to express their competencies in ways that facilitate the roles of persons in other parts of the organization'.

Decentralization helped to ensure that decision-making was a close to where the actual activities of the organization took place. Importantly, members of each component had both equity and parity. As Christman explained: 'In this instance, equity is defined as having a stake in the outcome, whereas parity means having equal or similar power with major influentials'.[136] In other word, the matrix sought to eliminate the bunker-like orientation that usually develops in large bureaucracies where individual departments are competing for scarce resources.

Joan LeSage, Chairperson of the Geriatric/Gerontological Nursing Department (GGND) for 17 years, has contributed the following insights into how the matrix model worked. The GGND was (and still is) situated in the Bowman Center. The Bowman Center is housed in a building (new in 1978) connected to the other Medical Center site by an elevated walkway. In accord with Christman's decentralization policy, there were built-in cupboards outside each room for individual patient supplies and records. Adhering to the intention of the matrix organization and true to his preferred management style, LeSage says Christman gave her great freedom to plan, implement, allocate resources and evaluate the care programs as they changed to meet new needs and philosophies of care. The equity and parity built into the matrix system facilitated LeSage's collaboration with both psychiatric and geriatric medicine when a new geropsychiatric unit was established. The matrix increased efficiency in the collection of quality assurance and program monitoring data across units such as rehabilitation, geropsychiatric, medical, even extending to nursing clinics in Chicago's Seniors Centers.[137]

Christman's reputation and his innovations at Rush attracted practitioners/teachers with clinical expertise in gerontological nursing at a time when such specialists were rare. Consequently, the Bowman Center became an excellent educational environment for undergraduates and postgraduates interested in care of the elderly. LeSage says she believed Christman valued her clinical specialist knowledge and like many of his colleagues she found him warm, frank and enthusiastic.[138]

The other plank in the raft of innovations that made up the Rush model was the unification of nursing service and education. At Rush, the unification of service and education was much more successful and went further than Christman's previous effort at Vanderbilt. Under his leadership, the divide that often existed between the nursing service and nursing education was virtually erased.

By the time of his appointments at Rush, nurses knew about the new philosophy and those who did not feel comfortable with it had already chosen to leave.[139] Nurses currently employed in the hospital were invited to apply for positions in the new school. But they had to meet the following criteria: have master's level preparation, a defined expertise in clinical practice and, vitally, be in tune with his unified practice plans.[140] Even though doctorate-prepared nurses were in short supply, in Christman's view they were essential. Only doctoral-prepared nurses had the required education and research experience to teach the clinical doctorate that he planned to implement.

Faith Jones was one of the doctoral-prepared nurses that Christman sought out. She was invited to spend two days at Rush. Ostensibly the invitation was enable her to see the innovations that Christman had made in the hope of persuading her to join the staff, since Jones was happy enough where she was. Christman arranged for her to meet key staff in the hospital and faculty. Only later did she become aware that the staff she met reported their opinions on her suitability to Christman. His employment strategy worked. Jones says it was Christman's commitment to the unification of service and education and the staff's enthusiasm that persuaded her to accept the offer and she stayed for four years. She remembers Christman as a charismatic leader, who expected faculty to get on with the implementation of his vision for nursing. In retrospect she thinks he was seldom disappointed because his enthusiastic expectations of staff performance helped ensure this. If a plan failed in some way, Jones remembered feeling that she had let him down, even when Christman assured her that she had done her best. A popular figure on campus, he was constantly out and about, always addressing people by name and showing interest in their personal welfare. Arriving well before office hours, the open door of his office always signaled an invitation to drop in and have a chat.[141]

Another well qualified nurse who 'succumbed to Luther's charm and persuasive powers to join the Rush community' was Dr Shirley Fondiller, who was then editor of *American Nurse*. She says that not being a clinician did not seem to bother him, since 'he was a risk-taker who hungered for new ideas and non-traditional approaches to doing things'. She remembers Christman saying to her: 'you have other skills and contributions to make. If you have an idea, try it out, if it doesn't work, you haven't lost anything'.[142]

By 1972, the first twenty-two faculty members were in place. As the School developed, the number of nurses with PhDs or master's degrees rose to 140 in 1978 becoming 280 in 1988.[143] Members of the faculty combined teaching and clinical practice, most spending two fifths of their time in the College and three fifths leading clinical units. There was some flexibility about the division of time depending on the clinical area of interest and some faculty only spent one day in a clinical unit. Nevertheless this was a far cry from the limited involvement in clinical work by educators in other institutions. In many schools of nursing, faculty sat in their office most of the day, making up exam questions, grading papers and preparing Lectures. Christman said that at Rush:

> There is no separation between service and education of nurses, so the whole enrichment of the environment of practice, teaching and research is a constant one, in all units all the time. This creates an entirely different kind of milieu from the more sterile milieu that is in most hospitals—where it's stuffily bureaucratic.[144]

Thus the strands of clinical practice, teaching, research and consultation became one—the integrated or unified role of a professional nurse. It was the fulcrum on which the unity of service and education rested. For Christman, it exemplified the highest quality of care and education delivery. It gave students expert tuition in the clinical units as well as the classroom. At Rush, faculty had the satisfaction of keeping their clinical skills up-to-date in their primary field of interest and in teaching clinical skills to students while they themselves were engaged in direct patient care. By practicing in this way, faculty members were behavioral models for students and young staff. In addition they had the advantage of conducting research in the hospital in which they taught and practiced. For Christman, this exemplified the professional role:

> The full use of knowledge is an obligation each profession owes to the clients it serves. Artificial constraints on full professional competence do a disservice to the public. The academic enterprise cannot remain encapsulated from the empirical utilization of knowledge, and the service system cannot remain insulated from the source of most knowledge and still produce professional

services that will be highly valued by society. When the
two elements are welded together in a unified whole, a
linkage system is in place for the rapid dissemination of
new knowledge [and] for the examination of novel and
more sophisticated practice issues .... [145]

A second integral part of the Rush model was the introduction
of nurse/physician teams. In the same way they had at Vanderbilt,
nurses and the physicians shared the responsibility for the care of a
specified group of patients—collaborative or associated practice are
other terms used to describe this innovation. As far as nursing was
concerned, associated practice naturally flows from the development
of primary nursing—the nurse meets all the needs of the patient,
from admission to discharge and works with physicians with the
same clinical focus.

Christman knew from his experience at Vanderbilt that a model
of shared power would enhance the care of both groups. For nurses
it required the same level of accountability as the physicians and
higher levels of preparation and for the physician it involved new
relationships and ways of working. As Christman pointed out 'Physicians will have to give thoughtful consideration as to how they
individually operate in the hospital system. ... In addition, they will
have to take time to participate in staff meetings in the units where
they have patients to help establish the best means to improve the
standards of care.'[146]

In a joint paper by the physicians and nurses involved in associated practice, the associate nurse's responsibilities are described as
an extension of a primary nurse role. Nurse associates may begin
by seeing patients in outpatients and then become the primary care
provider depending on each patient's needs. As far as inpatients are
concerned, all communication with others is through the predomi-

nant care nurse - thus this nurse is accountable for all care provided, including continuity of care from outpatient to inpatient. All medical orders go through resident medical staff, but in units where there is not a resident physician, a nurse associate may write orders, provided they are countersigned with 48 hours. Nursing histories are not separate since an integrated system of hospital records all patient progress notes together. [147]

Based on their experience at Rush, the physicians and nurses offered this advice on negotiating such a close relationship between the disciplines:

> … Several important aspects need to be discussed. These would include the nurse-physician collegial relationship, division of responsibilities, time commitment, financial reimbursement, and future professional goals for each person. … The nurse and physician must understand that questioning a colleague's approach to patient care is not an accusation of poor patient management: rather, it is a stimulus to growth of competence and better patient care.[148]

The objective of the nurse's role was the joint provision of care and 'not simply to make that of the physician easier', although it mostly turned out that way. Many nurses at Rush found their work very fulfilling but exacting. Christman says the turnover became 30 per cent compared to 65 per cent before primary nursing and associative practice was fully implemented. Most turnover occurred because Rush attracted young married nurses who left because of their husband's career or to undertake further study.[149]

Not unexpectedly, the Rush model raised concerns among faculty in other institutions. Whether involvement in practice was really necessary to successfully transmit knowledge to students was questioned. Fears that promotion and tenure would become linked to faculty practice were expressed.[150] For these reasons a lack of commitment to faculty practice was quite wide spread in the 1970s. [151] [152]

Although commitment to faculty practice was not lacking at Rush, some found it very demanding. The unification model stretched their personal resources to the full. Faith Jones says she had never worked so hard in any previous job.[153] As another nurse explained: 'This is more than simply a job, and people that are not interested in having a really professional career would not like it. It is really hard work.' A 'really professional career' at Rush had other rewards as well. According to Jones, parties among the staff were frequently held in the excellent restaurant maintained at Rush.[154] Despite the collegial atmosphere and the intrinsic rewards some found the unification model stressful. As another nurse pointed out: '... a setting which assigns so much responsibility for a really sick person to a specific nurse day after day really puts a great demand on the nurse, and especially on younger nurses'.[155]

Part of Christman's initial consultation period at Rush involved devising a new undergraduate curriculum. Since, in his view nursing is a marriage of science and humanism synthesized into an applied science with the entire rigor that this implies, Christman's first step was to develop an educational network with eight colleges in the region. This consortium provided a humanistic education and the basic behavioral and biological sciences necessary for entry. The colleges were also a source of potential students who were given priority acceptance into Rush programs. Importantly the agreement allowed Rush to have some control over the curriculum provided by the colleges.[156]

Building on his participatory management experience at Vanderbilt, he worked in consultation with existing faculty and they drew up a conceptual framework that emphasized science and its application to practice. Christman's views on nursing curricula are encapsulated in this statement:

> First, nursing must be conceptualized as an applied science. Second, the student must be educated as a generalist. Third, sciences cannot be conceived of as being static. They are a surging kind of phenomena. There is always new knowledge being poured into the system. To tie the three premises together a knowledge-link system must be the *modis operandi* of the curriculum design.[157]

The National League of Nursing accredited the new curriculum and it was ready for students in 1975. Naturally, a central feature was the behavioral models provided by practicing faculty in the clinical units. Over the next few years the curriculum underwent a number of revisions. Introductory research, pharmacology, and management subjects were added. But the basic objectives for the program remained the same: to provide competent practitioners for any field of clinical practice and an education that would articulate with graduate programs in clinical specialties.

As the undergraduate program got underway, a master's program was instituted. Most existing postgraduate programs prepared nurses for administration or education as already noted. As Christman kept repeating in addresses and publications, new knowledge was being created at a faster rate than could be translated into practice and one of the ways of overcoming this gap was to introduce advanced practice in clinical specialization.[158]

Once again he was able to build on his previous experience at Vanderbilt. At Rush, the clinical master's program allowed students to specialize in either medical/surgical, psychiatric or geriatric nursing. In line with Christman's thinking regarding the centrality of clinical practice, a clinical practicum was an important feature of the curriculum. This took place in two of the four quarters over which the program was run, and independent clinical studies were offered in the fourth.[159] In a deviation from the accepted norm for master's programs, a thesis was not required, although later on students who wanted research experience were offered that option.

When Christman had previously developed a clinical-focused master's program for nurse practitioners at Vanderbilt, it had not been well received by nursing leaders in Tennessee. Given this experience, he was not surprised to find that nursing leaders did not expect the Rush program to attract many students. How wrong they were. The program not only attracted students, it gained an international reputation.

For many years Christman had held the view that nurses would never achieve full professional status until all faculty held doctorates, since their image is dependent to a large extent on having the same preparation as other health professionals.[160] And, since the profession is an applied science he believed that clinical doctorates should be offered as well as the usual research-based degree such as the Doctor of Philosophy (PhD in nursing). Following hard on the heels of the master's program, a Doctorate of Nursing Science (DNSc) was introduced at Rush. A colleague described the program in detail. It 'included a core of basic sciences, such as physiology and behavioral science; a strong research emphasis with courses in the philosophy of science, theory, research design and methods, and statistics; in-depth physical assessment skills; and clinical hours and electives in the student's area of clinical research'.[161] The expectations were that graduates would 'develop the competencies of an expert clinical practitioner, have the investigative skills of a nurse researcher, and the leadership skills for developing health policy and changing health care systems'.[162] The first five students were admitted in 1977, and according to Christman, one of them was not a nurse but a physiologist.

Christman did not lose sight of his commitment to male nurses while at Rush. Men were about six percent of the 1800 staff at the hospital, nearly double the percentage of male nurses in the nursing workforce at the time.

The success of the Rush Model was due to a myriad of factors. Funding was one of the key components. Up to 1979, grants, gifts, endowments and capitation moneys amounted to more than nine and a half million. These included a Bush Foundation grant of $500,000 which funded the initial planning and implementation of the educational programs and added another $465,000 to expand the master's program and launch the clinical doctorate. In addition, a John L. and Helen Kellogg gift of $4,500,000 endowed the deanship and supported the establishment of a center for excellence in nursing.[163] Funding provided an impetus to unification plans and may have been a factor in the length of time unification models remained in place. The universities of Rush, Case Western Reserve and Rochester all received Kellogg grants, whereas Florida, the first to do away with the model, does not appear to have been so fortunate.

Two, under the combined leadership of Campbell and Christman at Rush the model was accepted at all levels throughout the institution—board, administration, service and faculties. Acceptance was facilitated by the matrix structure that gave staff a voice in policy and planning and this was central to the success of the Rush model of nursing.

Third, the way in which costs were distributed was certainly another factor. The Rush model was made economically practical by a scheme that split the salary costs between the patient care and the education budgets. In addition, since staff members were self-directed there were some savings in administrative costs. The distribution of costs enabled a very large highly educated staff to be employed. A normal teaching program of comparable size would have employed thirty to forty staff whereas Rush had over two hundred.[164]

There was one other very important ingredient. The Rush model gained international renown. Although this was largely due to its intrinsic qualities as a model of nursing practice, its reputation owed much to Christman's flair for energetic promotion. This took the form of two interrelated activities. One was the on-campus program on the Rush model conducted each year. High profile nurses from other countries were invited to attend. The other was his willingness to accept short teaching posts in other countries to lecture on the model. He taught in Sweden many times, Japan several times, and he lectured in Canada, New Zealand, Switzerland, Britain, Australia, Taiwan, Saudi Arabia and Turkey. In turn the aura of international success contributed to high staff morale and commitment at Rush.

Not content with these achievements Christman introduced a 'Plan for the 1990s'. The plan called for the following measures: discontinuation of undergraduate programs at Rush; entry into the profession to be raised to graduate level; eventual employment of only nurses with doctoral preparation; research programs, multidisciplinary appointments and consultancies to be started by all faculty; and, the encouragement of visiting scholars.[165]

On campus, the debate on baccalaureate entry level was revived. The faculty was diffident about such a move, concerned that state organizations were still debating the pros and cons of raising entry levels. The idea that the College of Nursing should become a graduate school was also resisted on the grounds that many postgraduate students were those from their own undergraduate programs. The latter was a very important point in a competitive education environment. Given Christman's college consortium strategy when setting up the original undergraduate program, he would have understood the importance of maintaining connections to the most likely source of graduates.

Since 1984 there had been widespread concern with the rising cost of health care in the USA. It was not only the high costs of new technology and changes in medical practices and therapies that was causing concern, it was also cost of the provision of nursing care and education. Rush was not exempt from these considerations and the requirement that all members of the faculty have doctoral preparation was the most 'explosive'.[166] As well, Christman thought that after completing the baccalaureate degree, nurses should continue their education through master's and doctoral level without stopping to obtain work experience.

Such radical ideas were bound to evoke criticism from many quarters. The faculty were sufficiently concerned to consult nurse leaders from other universities: Greta Styles, University of California; Rozelle Schloetfelt, Case Western Reserve University; and Judith Krause, Yale University. The heat was taken out of the controversy when Christman thought of several points of leverage and developed a new strategy, which he labeled the Implementation Plan. Since educational levels for education and practice were the main sticking points, implementation was to be by a series of articulated steps. Two features ensured this plan's success. One, implementation should proceed in stages and two, education programs would be flexible with multiple points of entry and exit.[167]

In the new plan, entry to graduate programs included those with baccalaureate degrees in nursing and also those with associate diplomas who displayed some evidence of graduate study potential. Entry to doctoral programs would also be flexible. Most importantly, in view of the faculty's concerns, those studying for a master's degree could exit at that point as a beginning specialist. The vote on these measures was taken and it came out in favor of the Implementation Plan. This occurred at Luther Christman's last faculty meeting; he had already tendered his resignation as the Dean and the Vice Chancellor of Nursing Affairs.

The years at Rush were indeed the highpoint of Christman's career. Many of changes tested in the original pilot study remain in place there today: doorside charting, common progress notes are examples. Even more important each RN is responsible for the total care of an individual patient. Fondiller, who worked closely with Christman for seven years, says it was the most fulfilling time of her professional life and his 'ideas, humanity and courage enriched us all'.[168] One of his favorite sayings was 'Nurses who think big, accomplish big things'[169] and Christman certainly did just that.

Another revered American nurse, Virginia Henderson, summed up his achievements at Rush in a letter to him:

> I have been impressed with your leadership ever since I knew you as Dean of Nursing at Vanderbilt University; but even more so as Dean/Vice President at Rush University. Like Annie W. Goodrich, another great nurse educator and administrator, you have asked for and been given the control of nursing service in a major hospital where your students learnt the practice of nursing. In this hospital students were taught by nurses who practice as well as teach. You have encouraged experi-

ments with unit management that promoted integration of education and service. ... Because of all this, and more, the Rush University Medical Center, in which your programs are based, is in every way, including architecturally, a showpiece of excellence in nursing. It is a center to which nurses, of this and other countries, come to see some of the very best of American nursing and nursing education. By this means and your consultation and teaching abroad, the Rush model has influenced nursing around the world.[170]

By the time he retired in 1987, Christman had become an icon and one of the most honored internationally recognized figures in American nursing.[171] In 1995 the American Academy of Nursing named Luther Christman a Living Legend and in 2004 he was inducted into the American Nurses' Association's Hall of Fame—the first male nurse to receive this honor.

Christman has not only received most of the highest accolades and awards nursing can bestow, but medicine and many other disciplines have recognized his contribution to scholarship and professional practice with numerous other awards and honorary doctorates. Two examples stand out. In 1979 he was made an honorary life time member by Alpha Omega Alpha (the medical honor society) for his advancement of clinical nursing throughout his career—the only nurse to be recognized in this way. In 1982, the American Association for the Advancement of Science made him a Fellow. This latter award is a prestigious acknowledgment of the quality of Christman's research and innovations in nursing and only one other nurse has received this honor.

These are remarkable achievements. When considered in the light of the gender discrimination that dogged Christman's career they are even more remarkable. It seems that the barriers put in his path increased his determination to institute his vision of nursing practice.

CHAPTER THIRTEEN

REFLECTIONS

B y the time he retired in 1987, Christman had become an icon and one of the most honored and internationally recognized 20th century figures in American nursing.[172] In the clinical, academic and administrative fields, Luther Christman has made a significant and widely acknowledged contribution to the profession of nursing. The story of his career shows that Christman was a re-markably effective administrator, strategic thinker and visionary. In addition to initiating the faculty practice model at Rush, Christman developed clinical programs that are now commonplace; two exam-ples are nurse practitioners and clinical doctoral degree programs. A provocative speaker, he was consistently sought after to present pa-pers at conferences. A prolific writer, he published numerous papers and wrote two books. Professional activities have included the es-tablishment of two national organizations, the Academy of Nursing and the National Academies of Practice. He played a significant part in the inauguration of the American Assembly for Men in Nursing (AAMN) and still holds the position of president.

Christman still vividly remembers the barriers put in his way and a sense of injustice could easily have become his Achilles heel. Given his mother's demeaning treatment, a lack of confidence could have bedeviled his professional life. Instead it gave him courage—since he had survived that treatment, other tribulations paled by comparison. Indeed, such obstacles and trials he did face seemed to fire his determination to succeed, while his optimism helped him survive his disappointments. Undoubtedly these characteristics played a large part in his success. As some of the incidents in this story of his professional life have illustrated, Christman is quick-witted and resourceful. His persuasiveness, coupled with the firm belief that any reasonable person would see the virtue of his arguments, helped engender commitment to his ideas from the various faculty with whom he worked. Quite early in his career he embraced a participatory management style and those to whom he delegated were expected to get on with the job with minimal interference—provided they in turn embraced his vision of nursing.

Christman challenged many long held traditions. Among those that stand out are multiple entry levels for registration and the employment of the least educated to give hands-on patient care. When facing entrenched tradition he drew on his research to convince others or demonstrated that his suggestions were based on sound commonsense. This is well illustrated by the changes to nursing curriculum and clinical practice he made and evaluated in the universities and hospitals where he worked.

Certainly at Rush Medical Center and University, the most highly educated and clinically skilled nurses worked in an equal partnership with physicians and had the authority and responsibility to perform nursing care tailored to the needs of individual patients. Nursing students were taught by academics engaged in clinical practice as well as teaching and research. Yet Christman's vision for nursing was not fully realized even at Rush—a nursing science degree as the minimum entry level for registration has not eventuated. Any radical change to the rules for registration requires the wholehearted support of state and federal nurses associations and in the 21st century this still seems unlikely. Christman might have been able to sway the debate on entry levels his way if he had been elected president of the ANA—who knows?

Thus although Christman successfully implemented his plans in the institutions where he held appointments, as far as the profession is concerned, many of the battles that he fought remain unresolved. As Ellen Baer, one of America's distinguished commentators on the nursing profession notes:

> As the twenty first century begins, nurses still struggle to attain autonomy for their profession, control of their practice, the right to independent decision-making, the determination of appropriate knowledge, education and licensure for various levels of nursing practice, nurse staffing levels that ensure patient safety and comfort, and salaries commensurate with nurses' responsibilities.[173]

Every leader has triumphs and disappointments. Reflecting on his career Christman acknowledges both. He now wishes he had published more on his research and the work he did on primary nursing and nurse/physician teams at Vanderbilt Hospital. Christman says that this was because he is more of an action man than a theorist; certainly much of his huge amount of published work in journals could be classified in academic terms as insightful opinion (rather than research) papers. Although his research informed his opinions, it is his mission and vision that appears to drive much of his writing.

Christman is naturally a promoter and publicist. As a speaker he was much sought after, partly because of his reputation as a controversial maverick. He is 'something of a grand old man of nursing in the US, lionized and anthologized and otherwise praised and [yet] blamed for his outspokenness'.[174] To some extent he has relished this reputation and it proved an asset. The number of invitations he accepted are a testament to both his popular appeal as a challenging and fluid speaker and his own enjoyment of this mode of delivery.

Regardless of all his achievements and accolades, the ANA election debacle clearly illustrated that regardless of the way in which a man had contributed to the nursing profession, many women felt that a man should not be allowed to head up one of the most influential nursing organizations. Certainly being 'a man with demonstrable drive' in woman's profession did lead to 'female chauvinism' and Christman says he found the feelings it evoked uncomfortable and difficult. His failure to be elected as president of the American Nurses Association was a frustrating disappointment—it effectively curtailed his influence at the national organizational level. Nevertheless his minority status as a 'male' nurse contributed to his success. An outsider by virtue of his gender, Christman evaded partisan squabbles and consistently stood back far enough to see the big picture.

The prejudice that Christman experienced from the beginning to the middle of his career can be explained, but scarcely justified, by the strong belief that nursing is a woman's only profession and that it needed to be defended against any possibility of male encroachment. The view that every man was ambitious by nature and craved power clearly worried women nursing leaders.

While there is still some discrimination against men in evidence, the fear of a male take-over of American nursing seems to have abated and anyway it is unlikely to be realized. In the 21st century men in leadership positions are still sufficiently rare to attract the headline 'Breaking Nursing Tradition' when it was announced that in 2003 that the first male president of Sigma Theta Tau International would be Daniel Pesut.[175] Given the few men in nursing in the USA and the difficulties in recruiting them, the possibility that enough men with such outstanding qualities as Pesut and Christman will collectively become a major influence in the profession remains remote.

Acknowledged leaders are frequently asked to predict the future of their profession. As befits a Living Legend the story of his career ends with a summary of Christman's thoughts on the future.

For more than twenty years, Christman has commented on the future of the nursing profession in a time of great scientific change in the post-industrial world of the knowledge society.[vii] In tracing the predictions he has made between 1978 to 2000, those associated with influence of technological changes and the knowledge revolution in health care have mostly come to pass. Unfortunately some of his prognostications about nursing, education, professional status and influence have not.

In 1978, Christman's predictions reflected the vision for nursing he put forward during most of his career. He thought that nursing would move towards self-governance and that all care would be given by registered nurses accountable for their practice.[176] He predicted that nurses would finally put their house in order and eliminated all the artificially created division in their ranks such as the division between education and service, and, of course, the three levels of education for registration.

By 1987, observing the rate of technological change and exponential growth of scientific knowledge, Christman was predicting an array of differences in the way patient care would be managed.

Computers would automatically monitor each patient's condition reducing errors of commission and omission and aiding quality assessments. He believed it was only a matter of time before it would be possible for renewal of licensure to be based on meeting nationally established norms of expert practice. He predicted that nurses, freed by automation from much of the ritual and routine paperwork, would have more time to acquire the skills needed 'to deal sensitively with the wide range of emotional reactions to illness expressed in patient behaviors'. Christman pointed out that the emphasis on 'episodic and crisis' management of illness was already changing to focus on health maintenance as another priority and as health care became more expensive more patients would be nursed at home. Therefore more nurses would become health educators of both patients and carers. 'Since nursing is an applied science ... transforming scientific knowledge into patient care will be a major concern'—a remark that is in accord with the evidence-based practice movement currently embraced by both nursing and medicine.

As each new spin-off from science and technology requires sophisticated knowledge, 'the social mandate for health care practice is preparation not at baccalaureate level but at higher levels'. By 1987 he was predicting that eventually a clinical doctorate would be the entry-level requirement:

vii. According to Böhme and Stehr (1986:23-24) the term 'knowledge society' first appears in an article, 'The decline of politics and ideology in a knowledgeable society', by Robert E.Lane in 1966 (American Sociological Review 31:650). It gained wide acceptance in 1973, when it was used by Daniel Bell, the author of The Coming of the Post-Industrial Society, New York: Basic Books.

> Launching a professional career is far different for persons who have a doctoral degree than for those who do not. The sheer satisfaction of having levels of knowledge similar to those of colleagues on the health team, the adequacy of that base for absorbing new knowledge, and the capability of using sophisticated methods of science are all intrinsic satisfactions that stimulate interest in the job.[177]

It is the expert clinicians who will have power, influence, and reap economic rewards. He again emphasized that: 'If nurses wish to have parity with other members of the health team, they must have equally rigorous clinical preparation ... otherwise they will not be able to influence the form and direction of the health care delivery system.[178]

By 2000, Christman was optimistically predicting that, by the time of adulthood, a lifestyle tied to health maintenance will be established for much of the population with even the aged having a reduced incidence of illness—resulting in a corresponding drop in the need for health care.[179] Which led Christman to a less hopeful prediction for the nursing profession. He warned that there could be a sharp reduction in demand for health care professionals and increased competition between professional groups:

> Regardless of the individual reaction of each nurse to the awesome developments in science, the inevitability of remarkable change confronts the profession. All of us must be aware of that reality. The best outcomes for patients and for nurses will be achieved if we are active in enriching knowledge as the basis of practice in proportion to the expansion of knowledge. Adjustments of

less quality will be maladaptive and make the future of nursing problematic.[180]

This in turn raises the question of the composition of the nursing workforce. Christman repeated his concern at the persistent recruitment of primarily white women. He sees that this as no longer viable, if it ever was, given the chronic staff shortages. Nevertheless he finds the position statement of the American Association of Colleges of Nursing encouraging. The statement calls for recruitment of both women and men of all races who have the desired intelligence and qualifications.

Christman again stressed the impact of the knowledge revolution—saying that, at a bare minimum, in twelve years there will be 128 times as much scientific evidence available—'knowledge being used to today will be obsolete tomorrow'.[181] Changes in technology have already altered the way in which hospital care is structured—many surgical procedures only require a day or less in hospital. Along with scientific commentators Christman foresees that genetic knowledge will radically alter disease profiles—schizophrenia, bipolar disorders, diabetes, cancer, and cardiac disorders are among those he cites. Genetic profiling will allow illness prevention to commence in infancy, so parents can be educated 'in the best way to manage the health of each child'.

The structure of care will necessarily change even more in the wake of medical science 'break-throughs':

> Most of the care may be in the home. Building access ramps, widening doorways and other akin adaptations to permit patients in wheel chairs to move freely will spark this goal. Remote palpation, automatic medication, monitoring devices, and on-line computer connections will enable home health nurses to function with

fewer and better-prepared nurses. Instead of visiting every patient, home health nurses will be able to use these devices to [visit only] when patients need the physical presence of a nurse. These nurses will be prepared at doctoral level. Computers will enhance the mode of care because they will be voice responsive: patients will not have to deal with the complexity of computer management in its present form.[182]

Computer networks will ensure that practitioners in every discipline, when faced with complex problems can easily consult specialists through a national list of identified experts.

Once this network is available, there will be strong ethical and legal imperatives to provide the best possible treatments for each patient. Health maintenance information will be taught in schools and academic programs and be available on the Internet.

Since his retirement in 1987, nursing has certainly experienced a number of changes, but often these are not in the directions that Christman worked for, nor are they those he predicted. Unfortunately multiple entry levels remain and anti-intellectualism is still rife. In a 2002 interview, Christman said he thinks there are indications American nursing is at last moving in the right direction, citing the increase in clinical master's and doctoral degrees and more gender-neutrality as examples.[183]

As the story of his career demonstrates, in his administrative and academic roles Christman has been a practical man of action, but when pursuing his vision for the future of nursing he is, and always has been, an optimistic idealist at heart. Even if, as Christman hopes, nursing is starting to move in the directions he so strongly advocates, 'it is unlikely to be far enough or fast enough to suit this tenacious and determined leader'.[184]

ENDNOTES

Chapter One: Christman's First Campaign

[1] Kalisch, P.A. and Kalisch, B.J. (1995). *The advance of American nursing*. 3rd Ed. Philadelphia: J.B. Lippincott, p. 401.

[2] Craig, L.N. (1940). Opportunities for Men Nurses. *American Journal of Nursing*, 40(6): 666-670.

[3] Kalisch, P.A. and Kalisch, B.J. note 1, p.403.

[4] Walsh, M.R. (1977). *Doctors wanted: No women need apply: Sexual barriers in the medical profession 1835–1975*. New Haven: Yale University Press, pp. 218–9.

[5] Frances Payne Bolton School of Nursing, Case Western Reserve University Web page: About Frances Payne Bolton. http://www.cwru.edu. [Accessed 22 June 2005]

Chapter Two: Growing up

[6] Pennsylvania Hospital Historical Timeline, 1914–65. http://www.uphs.upenn.ed/paharc/timeline [Accessed 12 September 2003]

[7] Merrill, S.E. (1998). *Luther Christman: Professional reformer*. Doctoral thesis, University of Michigan, Michigan, pp. 47-8.

[8] Pennsylvania Hospital Historical Timeline, note 6.

[9] Craig, L. note 2, p. 12.

[10] McCleland, H. (1952) Reference letter for Christman titled 'To whom it may Concern'. From the Luther Christman Collection in The Howard Gottlieb Research Center at Boston University, Ma.

[11] Pennsylvania School of Nursing for Men, Philadelphia (1939). *Maltesan*. Published in honor of the Founders of the School by the graduating class of 1939.

[12] Lysaught, J.P. (1978). A *Luther Christman anthology* , Nursing Digest Special Issues VI (2): 6-7.

[13] Craig, L. (1952). Reference for Luther Christman. From the Luther Christman Collection in The Howard Gottlieb Research Center at Boston University, Ma.

[14] Nadig, G.K. (1952). Reference for Luther Christman from the Adviser, Department of Nursing, Temple University, December 1. From the Luther Christman Collection in The Howard Gottlieb Research Center at Boston University, Ma.

Chapter Four: Mental Health and Other Arenas

[15] Christman, L. (1988). Luther Christman. In Schorr, T.M. and Zimmerman, A.: *Making choices, taking chances: Nurse leaders tell their stories*. St Louis: Mosby, pp 43–52.

[16] Christman, L. and Counte, M.A. (1981). *Hospital organization and health care delivery*. Colorado: Westview Press.

[17] Senge, P. (1992). The fifth discipline: *The art and practice of the learning organization*. London: Nicholas Brealey Publishing.

[18] Bruget, D. (1956). Who's to Blame for Fuss at the Hospital? Article in *Yankton Press and Dakotan*, probably January or February. Luther Christman's personal archives. (Incomplete heading).

[19] Schutt, B.C. (1968) Editorial. *American Journal of Nursing*, 68(7): 1455.

[20] Kalisch and Kalisch, note 1, p. 372.

[21] Bullough V.L. and Bullough, B. (1969). *The emergence of modern nursing*. London: Macmillan, p.228.

[22] Christman, note 15, p. 47.

[23] Christman, note 15, p. 49.

Chapter Five: The Entry Level Debate

[24] Christman, L. (1976b). Leadership Style and Organisational Effectiveness. Paper given at the Shirley Titus Lecture, California Nurses' Association Convention,

Los Angeles, California, 9 March. This paper is substantively the same as that titled 'Nursing Leadership—Style and Substance', published in the *American Journal of Nursing*, 67(10), October, 1967.

[25] Lusk, B., Russell, R.L., Rodgers, J. & Wilson-Branett, J. (2001). Preregistration Nursing Education in Australia, New Zealand, the United Kingdom, and the United States of America. *Journal of Nursing Education*, 40 (5): 200.

[26] Lynaugh, J.E. (2001). Nursing's History: Looking Backward and Seeing Forward. In Baer, E.D., D'Antonio, P., Rinker, S. and Lynaugh, J.E. (eds), *Enduring issues in American nursing*. New York: Springer, p. 20.

[27] Porter, E. (1963). Traditions and Realities. In Money and Nursing, a special supplement, *American Journal of Nursing*, 63(11): M-6.

[28] Marquis, B., Lillibridge, J. and Madison, J. (1993). Problems and Progress as Australia Adopts the Bachelor's Degree as the Only Entry to Practice. *Nursing Outlook*, May/June: 136.

[29] Lusk, B., et al, note 25, p. 196.

[30] Lusk. B., et al, note 25, p. 201.

[31] *American Journal of Nursing* (1900). Editor's Miscellany. Volume 1(1), October: 60.

[32] Brown, E.L. (1965). Preparation for Nursing. *American Journal of Nursing*, 65(9): 70.

[33] Christman, L. and Kirkman, R.E. (1972). A Significant Innovation in Nursing Education. In Lysaught, J.P. (Ed) (1978) A *Luther Christman anthology*. Massachusetts: A Nursing Digest/Contemporary Publication, p. 33. (Reprinted from *Peabody Journal of Education*, 30(10), October, 1972.)

[34] Porter, E., note 27, p. M-5.

[35] Sutherland, D. (1963). Money at the bedside. In Money and Nursing, a special supplement, *American Journal of Nursing*, 63(11): M-8.

[36] Carter, M. (1988). The Professional Doctorate as an Entry Level to Practice. In *Perspectives in nursing*—1987—1989. Based on a presentations at the eighteenth NLN biennial convention. National League of Nursing Publication: p. 51.

[37] Christman, L. (1966b). Clinical Nursing - The Specialist - The Generalist. Paper presented at the Forty-Fifth Annual Meeting of the New England Hospital Assembly, Boston, March 30, pp. 165–6.

[38] Hubbard, W.N. (1965). Letter to Christman regarding three of Christman's articles on nursing. From the Luther Christman Collection in The Howard Gottlieb Research Center at Boston University, Ma, p. 2.

[39] Lysaught, J.P. (1978). Christman present: an interview on a life's career in nursing

leadership. In Lysaught, J.P. (ed), A *Luther Christman anthology*. A Nursing Digest Contemporary Publication, p. 8.

[40] King, S. (1965)Letter to the Editor. *American Journal of Nursing*, 65(9): 77-78.

[41] Driver. B. (1965). Letter to the Editor. *American Journal of Nursing*, 65(2): 63.

[42] Moore, R.J. (1965). Letter to the Editor. *American Journal of Nursing*, 65(4): 53.

[43] Nichols, E.F. (1997). Educational Patterns in Nursing. In Chitty, K.K. (Ed), *Professional nursing: Concepts and challenges, 2nd Ed*. Philadelphia: W.B. Saunders, pp. 37–8.

[44] Lysaught, J.P., note 39, p. 9.

[45] Schwirian, P. and Moloney, M.M (1998). *Professionalization of nursing: Current issues and trends, 3rd Ed*. Philadelphia: Lippincott, p. 24.

[46] Fondiller, S.H. (1999). Nursing Education in the 1960s: Revolt and Reform. *Nursing and Health Care Perspectives*, 20 (4): 182–3.

[47] National Commission for the Study of Nursing and Nursing Education (1970). *An Abstract for Action* by Jerome P. Lysaught. New York: McGraw-Hill.

[48] National Commission for the Study of Nursing and Nursing Education (1973). From *Abstract into Action* by Jerome P. Lysaught. New York: McGraw-Hill.

[49] Lysaught, J.P. (1981). *Action in affirmative: Towards an unambiguous profession of nursing*. New York: McGraw-Hill.

[50] McClosky, J.C. (1981). Nursing Accreditation: to What End? In McClosky, J.C. and Grace, H.K. (Eds) *Current issues in nursing*, London: Blackwell Scientific Publications, p. 369.

[51] Christman, L. (1979a). B.S.N - The Entry Level for Practice. Paper presented at the 7th Annual Convention of the National Intravenous Therapy Association, Chicago, Illinois, June 13.

[52] Christman, L. (1966a). New Knowledge, New Technology, Demand New Practice. *Minnesota Nursing Accent*, Minnesota, December, pp. 153,166. Luther Christman personal archives.

[53] Christman, L., note 51.

Chapter Six: Advancing Nursing Practice

[54] Hamilton, D. (2001). Constructing the Mind of Nursing. In Baer, E.D., D'Antonio, P., Rinker, S. and Lynaugh, J.E. (eds), *Enduring issues in American nursing*. New York: Springer, pp. 244.

[55] Hamilton, D. note 54, pp. 312–3.

[56] Christman, L. and Counte, M.A., note 16, p. 17.

[57] Christman, L. (1965). *The Selective Perceptions Resulting from Training for a Vertical Division of Labor and the Effect on Organizational Cohesion*. Doctoral thesis, Michigan State University.

[58] Christman, L. (1976a). Prerequisite for Nurse-Physician Collaboration: Nursing Autonomy. Reported as panel response and audience interaction at a program sponsored by the National Joint Practice Commission, American Nurses' Convention, Atlantic City, in *Nursing Administration Quarterly*, 1 (1) June.

[59] Fondiller, S.H. (1984). Pattern for Unification. *Nursing Mirror*, 159(15): 23-24.

[60] Sutherland, D., note 35, M-9.

[61] Fairman, J. (2001). Delegated by Default or Negotiated by Need? Physicians, Nurse Practitioners, and the Process of Clinical Thinking. In Baer, E.D., D'Antonio, P., Rinker, S. and Lynaugh, J.E. (Eds), *Enduring issues in American nursing*. New York: Springer, pp. 313.

[62] Chitty, K.K. (1997). *Professional nursing: Concepts and challenges*. Philadelphia: W.B. Saunders, p. 288.

[63] Georgopoulos, B. and Christman, L. (1990). *The effects of clinical nursing specialization: A controlled organizational experiment*. New York: Edwin Mellen Press.

[64] Unnamed Author (1998). Letter dated 31 July to Aspen Publishers regarding the publication of collected papers of Luther Christman. (Luther Christman personal archives).

[65] Schwirian, P. and Moloney, M.M, note 45, p. 249.

[66] Christman and Kirkman, note 33, p. 34.

[67] Christman, L. (1971). *The Vanderbilt*, Vol 1 (1) Spring: 3.

[68] Fairman, J., note 61, pp. 311; 213.

[69] Fairman, J., note 61, p. 324.

[70] Fairman, J, note 61, p. 324.

[71] Sullivan, E. (2002). In a Woman's World. *Reflections on Nursing Leadership, Honor Society of Nursing, Sigma Theta Tau International*, Third Quarter, 28(3): 32.

[72] Sullivan, E. note 71, p. 32.

Chapter Seven: The Integration of Blacks

[73] Kalisch, P.A. and Kalisch,B.J., note 1, pp. 396–7.

[74] Bigham, G.D. (1964). To Communicate with Negro Patients. *American Journal of Nursing*, 64(9): 113–115.

Chapter Eight: Hitting a Glass Ceiling

[75] Merrill, S.E., note 7, p. 104.

[76] Lysaught, J.P., note 39, p. v.

[77] Christman, L., note 24, p. 3.

[78] Jones, F. (2003). Interview conducted by author, February.

[79] Fenski, M. (1971). Copy of a letter to Provost, Nicholas Hobbs, Vanderbilt University sent to Christman by Fenski. Luther Christman's personal archives.

[80] Fondiller, S.F. (2003) Personal communication with author.

[81] *American Journal of Nursing* (1968) Resumes of delegates. 68(3): 565.

[82] *American Journal of Nursing* (1968). Report on the convention. 68(6): 1271.

[83] Jackson, V.S. (1968). Letter to editor 'Resolution at Odds'. *American Journal of Nursing*, 68(9): 2112 and 2114.

[84] Lysaught, J.P., note 12, p. 5.

[85] Lysaught, J.P., note 12, p. 5–6.

Chapter Nine: Women's Domination of Nursing

[86] Dock, L.L. and Stewart, I.M. (1938). *A short history of nursing: From the earliest times to the present day*, 4th Ed. New York: G.P. Putnam's Sons. p. 368.

[87] Kalisch, P.A. and Kalisch, B.J., note 1, pp. 574–581.

[88] Bullough V.L. and Bullough, B., note 21. pp. 312–327.

[89] Roberts, M.M. (1954). *American nursing: history and interpretation*. New York: Macmillan, pp. 312–327.

[90] Bexar County Archives & Nursing in Texas: A Pictorial History p. 56. http://www.geocities.com/Athens/forum/6011/sld)12.htm [Accessed 1 July 2005]

[91] Jamieson, E.M., Sewall, M.F. and Suhrie, E.B. (1966). *Trends in nursing history: Their social, international, and ethical relationships*, 6th Ed. Philadelphia: W.B. Saunders, p. 364.

[92] Dock, L.L. and Stewart, I.M. note 86, p. 401.

[93] Mottus, J.E. (1981). *The New York Nightingales: The emergence of the nursing pro-*

fession at Bellevue and New York Hospital 1850–1920. Ann Arbor: UMI Research Press, p. 71.

[94] Mottus, J.E. note 93, pp. 161–176.

[95] Craig L. note 12, pp. 666–670.

[96] Lewenson, S.B. (1996). *Taking charge: nursing, suffrage and feminism in America, 1873–1920.* New York: NLN Press, pp. 160–165.

[97] Lewenson, S.B. note 96, p. 163.

[98] Reverby, S.M. (1987) *Ordered to care: The dilemma of American nursing, 1850–1945.* Cambridge: Cambridge University Press, p. 51.

Chapter Ten: 20th Century Discrimination

[99] Melosh, B. (1982). *"The physician's hand": work, culture and conflict in American nursing.* Philadelphia: Temple University Press, p. 12.

[100] Snodgrass, M.E. (1999). *Historical encyclopedia of nursing*, Santa Barbara, California: ABC-CLIO, Inc.

[101] Care, D., Gregory, D., English, J. and Venkatesh, P (1996). A Struggle for Equality: Resistance to Commissioning Men in the Canadian military, 1952–1967. *Canadian Journal of Nursing Research* 28(1): 15.

[102] Editorial (1961). Men in Nursing. *American Journal of Nursing*, 61(2): 51

[103] Snodgrass, M.E. note 100.

[104] Halloran, E.J. (1985). Men in Nursing. In McClosky, J.C. and Grace, H.K. (Eds.), *Current issues in nursing*, St. Louis: Mosby, pp. 970–978.

[105] Foreman, M. (1997). Are Men Taking Over the Nursing Profession? *Contemporary Nurse*, 6 (1): 26–29.

[106] Lodge, N., Mallett, J. Blake, P. and Fryatt, I. (1997) A Study to Ascertain Gynaecological Patients' Perceived Levels of Embarrassment with Physical and Psychological Care Given by Female and Male Nurses, *Journal of Advanced Nursing* 25(5): 894.

[107] Halloran, E.J. and Welton, J.M. (1994). Why Aren't There More Men in Nursing? In McClosky, J.C. and Grace, H.K. (Eds.), *Current issues in nursing* (4th Ed), St. Louis: Mosby, pp. 684–691, and Porter, S. (1995). *Nursing's relationship with medicine: Critical realist ethnography.* Aldershot, UK: Ashgate Publishing, p. 100.

[108] Pittman, E. (1985). Goodbye, Florence: the nurses' struggle for status has ended the age of Florence Nightingale. *Australian Society*, February: 8–10.

[109] MacPhail, J. (1996). Men in Nursing. In Kerr, J.R. and MacPhail, J. *Canadian*

nursing: Issues and perspectives, 3rd Ed. St. Louis: Mosby. pp. 75–81.

[110] Bush, P.J. (1976). Male Nurse: A Challenge to Traditional Role Identities. *Nursing Forum* XV (4): 390–405; Skivington, S. and Dawkes, D. (1988). Fred Nightingale. *Nursing Times*, 84:49–51; Dassen, R., Nijhius, F. and Philipsen, H. (1990). Male and Female Nurses in Intensive Care Wards in the Netherlands. *Journal of Advanced Nursing*, 15: 387–394; Williams, C. (1992). The Glass Escalator: Hidden Advantages for Men in "Female" Professions. *Social Problems*, 39: 253–267; Perkins, J.L., Bennett, D.N. and Dorman, R.E. (1993). Why Men Choose Nursing. *Nursing and Health Care*, 14(1): 34–38.

[111] Streubert, H.J. (1994). Male Nursing Students' Perceptions of Clinical Experience. *Nurse Educator*, 19: 28–32.

[112] Brough, S. (2001). Why Men and Women Choose Nursing. *Nursing and Health Care Perspectives*, 22 (1), January/February.

[113] Halloran, E.J., note 104, pp. 970–978.

[114] American Nurses Association. (1963). Nurses ... Numbers and Characteristics. *American Journal of Nursing*, 63(1): 100–103.

[115] Christman, L. (1970). Maleness - One Means to Efficiency in Patient Care. Paper presented at the 1st Biennial Kenneth T. Crummer Lecture, Alumni Association of Pennsylvania Hospital School of Nursing for Men, March 18, Philadelphia.

[116] Halloran, E.J. and Welton, J.M., note 107, p. 690.

[117] Christman, L., note 51. p. 53.

[118] Williams, C. (1995). *Still a man's world: Men who do women's work*. Berkeley: University of California Press.

[119] Christman, L., note 15, pp. 43–52.

[120] Medzilla (2002). Medzilla Asks: Is Affirmative Action Required in the Nursing Field? News Release, June, page 1, http://www.medzilla.com [Accessed 11 September 2003]

[121] Christman, note 15, pp. 43–52.

Chapter Eleven: Raising Nursing's Profile

[122] NurseWeek.com (2002). Daniel Pesut, on Sigma Theta Tau International http://www.nurseweek.com/5min/pesut [Accessed 30 June 2005]

[123] *American Journal of Nursing* (1964). Changing ANA to Meet Challenging Needs, PII, Concern with practice, 64(4): 115.

[124] *Nursing Outlook* (1964). Report of the American Nurse's Association. 64(7): 41.

[125] Elliot, J.E., Zimmerman, A., Paulson, V.M. and Schlotfeldt, R. (1968). A conversation with: Jo Eleanor Elliot, Anne Zimmerman, Virginia M. Paulson, and Rozelle Schlotfeldt. *American Journal of Nursing*, 68(4): 798.

[126] American Academy of Nursing criteria for membership on Web site: http://www.nursingworld.org/aan/fellowship [Accessed 22 June 2005]

[127] Lysaught, J.P., note 39, pp. 9–10.

[128] Hilton, L. (2001). A Few Good Men. *NurseWeek*, 14 May: 1–4.

[129] Lewis, M.C. (1998). Men in Nursing: A Time for Re-evaluation. *Interaction*: 9–11.

[130] Henderson, V. (1978). Letter to Luther Christman. Luther Christman's personal archives.

Chapter Twelve: The Rush Model of Nursing

[131] Fisli, B.A. (1994). *The History of the Rush University, College of Nursing and the Development of the Unification Model, 1972–1988*. Doctoral thesis, Loyola University, Chicago, pp. 149-7; 233.

[132] *Urban Health* (1980). Article titled 'Primary Nursing at Rush-Presbyterian-St. Luke's Hospital', p. 30.

[133] Personal Communication, 16 September, 2003. p. 1. The section on the state of nursing care and the pilot study is drawn almost entirely from a communication from a nurse who did not give her full name.

[134] Personal communication, note 133, p. 2.

[135] Personal communication, note 133, pp. 4–5.

[136] Christman, L. (1980). An Organizational Perspective for Nursing Practice. Paper presented at the American Nurses' Association Convention, Houston, Texas, June 9–13, p.1.

[137] LeSage, J. (2003). Personal communication with the author. 16 September.

[138] LeSage, J. note 137.

[139] Fisli, note 131, p. 163.

[140] Fisli, note 131, p. 171–4.

[141] Jones, F. (2003). Interview with author, February.

[142] Fondiller, S.H. (2003). Correspondence with author, March.

[143] Christman, L. (2002). College of Nursing, Rush University statistics dated October. All headings to the tables are missing. (Luther Christman's personnel archives).

[144] *Urban Health*, note 132, p. 31.

[145] Christman, L. (1978). Doctoral Education: A Shot in the Arm for the Nursing Profession. In Lysaught, J.P. (ed) A *Luther Christman anthology*. Massachussetts: A Nursing Digest/Contemporary Publication. Reprinted from *Health Services Manager*, May 1977.

[146] Christman, L. (1979c). A Center of Excellence in the Making. Paper presented at Rush-Presbyterian-St. Luke's Medical Center, Chicago, at the Dedication of the John L. and Helen Kellogg Center of Excellence, p. 28.

[147] Elpern, E.H., Rodts, M.F., DeWald, R.L. and West, J.W. (1983). Associative Practice: A Case of Professional Collaboration. *The Journal of Nursing Administration*, November: p. 31.

[148] Elpern, E.H. et al., note 147, p. 28.

[149] *Urban Health*, note 132, p.35.

[150] Holm, K., Inman, S.L. and Ward, T.L.V. (1997). Critique of Christman on Leadership in Practice. *Image: Journal of Nursing Scholarship*, 29(2): 31.

[151] Diers, D. (1980). Faculty Practice: Models, Methods and Madness. In National League for Nursing Publication. No. 15–183, *Cognitive dissonance: Interpreting and implementing faculty practice roles in nursing education*. New York: National League for Nursing, pp. 7–15.

[152] Chicadonz, G., Bush, E., Kothuis, K., and Utz, S. (1981). Mobilizing Faculty Toward Integration of Practice into Faculty Roles. *Nursing & Health Care*, 2(12): 548–553.

[153] Jones, note 141.

[154] Jones, note 141.

[155] *Urban Health*, note 132, p. 34.

[156] Fisli, B.A., note 131, pp. 177–9.

[157] Christman, L. and Kirkman, R.E., note 33, p. 34.

[158] Christman, L. (1966b). note 37, p. 7.

[159] Fisli, B.A., note 131, p. 203.

[160] Christman, L., note 146, p. 45.

[161] Personal communication with a colleague of Christman's at Rush University, 16

September, 2003.

[162] Fisle, B.A., note 131, p. 212.

[163] Christman, L., note 146, p. 8.

[164] Merrill, S.E., note 7, p.122.

[165] Fisli, B.A., note 131, pp. 219–20.

[166] Fisli, B.A., note 131, p. 221.

[167] Fisle, B.A., note 131, p. 223–6.

[168] Fondiller, S.H. (2003). Email correspondence with the author, March.

[169] Christman, L., note 163.

[170] Henderson, V. (1987). Personal letter to Christman. (Luther Christman's personal acrchive).

[171] Sullivan, E., note 71, p. 10.

[172] Sullivan, E., note 71, p.10.

Chapter Thirteen: Reflections

[173] Baer, E.D. (2001). Introduction. In Baer, E.D., D'Antonio, P., Rinker, S. and Lynaugh, J.E., (Eds) *Enduring issues in American nursing*, New York: Springer Publications, p. 5.

[174] Bowman, J. (1978), *Good Medicine*. Chicago: Rush-Presbyterian-St. Luke's Medical Center, pp. 172–175.

[175] Cuthbertson, K. (2002) Breaking Nursing Tradition. *Indianapolis Business Journal*, 22 (47).

[176] Lysaught, J.P., note 12, pp. 16-17.

[177] Christman, L. (1987). The Future of the Nursing Profession. *Nursing Administration Quarterly*, 11 (2): 1–8.

[178] Christman, L., note 177, pp. 2–5.

[179] Christman, L. (2000). Management Adjustment—A Glimpse into the Future Structure of Care. *Nursing Administration Quarterly*, 25(1): 3.

[180] Christman, L., note 177, p.8.

[181] Christman, L., note 177, pp.1-3.

[182] Christman, I., note 177, p. 2.

[183] Sullivan, note 71, pp. 16–7.

[184] Sullivan, note 71, 17.

REFERENCES

American Academy of Nursing criteria for membership. Web site: http://www. nursingworld.org/aan/honfello3.htm#criteria [Accessed 22 July 2005]

American Journal of Nursing (1968). Report on the convention. 68(6): 1271.

American Journal of Nursing (1968). Resumes of delegates. 68(3): 565.

American Journal of Nursing (1990). Editor's Miscellany. 1(1), October: 60.

American Nursing Association (1963). Nurses ... numbers and characteristics. *American Journal of Nursing,* 63 (1):100–103.

Baer, E.D. (2001). Introduction. In Baer, E.D., D'Antonio, P., Rinker, S. and Lynaugh, J.E. (Eds.), *Enduring issues in American nursing.* New York: Springer, pp. 5–9.

Baer, E.D. and Gordon, S. (1994). Gender battle in nursing. *Boston Globe,* December 28:15.

Baer, E.D., D'Antonio, P., S. Rinker, and J.E. Lynaugh, (Eds.) 2001. *Enduring issues in American nursing.* New York: Springer.

Baly, M.E. (1995). *Nursing and social change.* London: Routledge.

Bigham, G. D. (1964). To communicate with Negro patients. *American Journal of Nursing,* 64 (9):113–115.

BÖhme, G. and Stehr, N. (Eds.) (1986). *The knowledge society: The growing impact of scientific knowledge on social relations.* Dordrecht: Holland.

Bowman, J. (1978). *Good medicine.* Chicago: Rush-Presbyterian-St. Luke's Medical Center.

Brough, S. (2001). Why men and women choose nursing. *Nursing and Health Care Perspectives*, 22 (1).

Brown, E.L (1965). Preparation for nursing. *American Journal of Nursing*, 65(9): 70

Bruget, D. (1956). Who's to blame for fuss at the Hospital? Article in *Yankton Press and Dakotan*, probably January or February (incomplete copy). (Christman's personal archives).

Bullough V.L. and Bullough, B. (1969). *The emergence of modern nursing.* London: Macmillan.

Bush, P.J. (1976). Male nurse: A challenge to traditional role identities. *Nursing Forum XV* (4): 390–405.

Care, D., Gregory, D., English, J. and Venkatesh, P. (1996). A struggle for equality: Resistance to commissioning men in the Canadian military, 1952-1967. *Canadian Journal of Nursing Research*, 28(1): 15.

Carnegie, M.E. (2001) Black nurses in the United States: 1879–1992. In Hein, E.C. (Ed.), *Nursing in the 21st century: Perspectives from the literature.* Philadelphia: Lippincott, pp. 122–134.

Carter, M. (1988). The professional doctorate as an entry level to practice. In *Perspectives in nursing—1987—1989.* Based on presentations at the eighteenth NLN biennial convention. National League of Nursing Publication: pp. 49–52.

Chalmers, D.M. (1965). *Hooded Americanism: The first century of the Ku Klux Klan, 1865–1965.* New York: Doubleday & Company.

Chicadonz, G., Bush, E., Kothuis, K., and Utz, S. (1981). Mobilizing faculty toward integration of practice into faculty roles. *Nursing & Health Care*, 2(12): 548-553.

Chinn, P.L. (1994). *Developing the discipline: Critical studies in nursing history and professional issues.* Gaithersburg, Maryland: Aspen.

Chitty, K.K. (1997). *Professional nursing: Concepts and challenges.* Philadelphia: W.B. Saunders.

Christman, L. (1965). *The selective perceptions resulting from training for a vertical division of labor and the effect on organizational cohesion.* Unpublished doctoral thesis, Michigan State University.

Christman, L. (1966a). New knowledge, new technology, demands new practice. *Minnesota Nursing Accent*, Minnesota, December: 53 (Christman's personal Archives)

Christman, L. (1966b). Clinical nursing - the specialist - the generalist. Paper presented at the Forty-Fifth Annual Meeting of the New England Hospital Assembly, Boston, March 30.

Christman, L. (1970). Maleness - one means to efficiency in patient care. Paper presented at the 1st Biennial Kenneth T. Crummer Lecture, Alumni Association of Pennsylvania Hospital School of Nursing for Men, March 18, Philadelphia.

Christman, L. (1971) *The Vanderbilt*, Vol 1(1) spring.

Christman, L. (1972). Baccalaureate programs and health care. Paper delivered at the 1972 annual meeting of the Association for Academic Health Centers, Dorado Beach, Puerto Rico, October 14.

Christman, L. (1976a). Prerequisite for nurse-physician collaboration: nursing autonomy. Reported as panel response and audience interaction at a program sponsored by the National Joint Practice Commission, American Nurses' Convention, Atlantic City, in *Nursing Administration Quarterly*, 1(1): 52.

Christman, L. (1976b). Leadership style and organizational effectiveness. Paper at the Shirley Titus Lecture, California Nurses' Association Convention, Los Angeles, California, 9 March. This paper is substantively the same as that titled 'Nursing leadership—style and substance', published in *American Journal of Nursing*, 67(10), October, 1967.

Christman, L. (1978). Doctoral education: A shot in the arm for the nursing profession. In Lysaught, J.P. (Ed.) *A Luther Christman anthology*. Massachusetts: A Nursing Digest/Contemporary Publication. Reprinted from *Health Services Manager*, May 1977.

Christman, L. (1979a). B.S.N - the entry level for practice. Paper presented at the 7th Annual Convention of the National Intravenous Therapy Association, Chicago, Illinois, June 13.

Christman, L. (1979b). New roles for personnel: nurses and physician extenders. *Bulletin New York Academy of Medicine*, 55 (1), pp 37–40.

Christman, L. (1979c). A center of excellence in the making. Paper presented at Rush-Presbyterian-St. Luke's Medical Center, Chicago, at the Dedication of the John L. and Helen Kellogg Center of Excellence.

Christman, L. (1980). An organizational perspective for nursing practice. Paper presented at the American Nurses' Association Convention, Houston, Texas, June 9–13.

Christman, L. (1987). The future of the nursing profession. *Nursing Administration Quarterly*, 11 (2):1–8.

Christman, L. (1988). Luther Christman. In Schorr, T.M. and Zimmerman, A. *Making choices, taking chances: Nurse leaders tell their stories.* St Louis: Mosby. pp 43–52.

Christman, L. (2000). Management adjustment—a glimpse into the future structure of care. *Nursing Administration Quarterly*, 25(1):1–4.

Christman, L. and Counte, M.A. (1981). *Hospital organization and health care delivery.* Colorado: Westview Press.

Christman, L. and Kirkman, R.E. (1978). A significant innovation in nursing education. In Lysaught, J.P. (Ed.) *A Luther Christman anthology.* Massachusetts: A Nursing Digest/Contemporary Publication. (Reprinted from *Peabody Journal of Education*, 30 (10), October, 1972.)

Craig, L.N. (1940). Opportunities for men nurses. *American Journal of Nursing*, 40 June: 666-670.

Craig, L.N. (1952). Reference for Luther Christman. The Luther Christman collection, Howard Gottlieb Research Center, Boston University, Ma.

Dassen, R., Nijhius, F. and Philipsen, H. (1990). Male and female nurses in intensive care wards in the Netherlands. *Journal of Advanced Nursing*, 15: 387–394.

Diers, D. (1980). Faculty practice: models. Methods and madness. In NLN Publication no. 15–183, *Cognitive dissonance: Interpreting and implementing faculty practice roles in nursing education.* New York: National League for Nursing, pp. 7-15.

Dock, L.L. and Stewart, I.M. (1938). *A short history of nursing: From the earliest times to the present day, 4th Ed.* New York: G.P. Putnam's Sons.

Driver, B. (1965). Letter to the editor. *American Journal of Nursing*, 65(2): 63.

Editorial (1961). Men in nursing. *American Journal of Nursing*, 6(2): 51.

Elliot, J.E., Zimmerman, A., Paulson, V.M. and Schlotfeldt, R. (1968). A conversation with: Jo Eleanor Elliot, Anne Zimmerman, Virginia M. Paulson, Rozelle Schlotfeldt. *American Journal of Nursing*, 68(4): 792-799.

Elpern, E.H., Rodts, M.F., DeWald, R.L. and West, J.W. (1983). Associative practice: a case of professional collaboration. *The Journal of Nursing Administration*, 83(11): pp.27–31.

Fairman, J. (2001). Delegated by default or negotiated by need? Physicians, nurse practitioners, and the process of clinical thinking. In Baer, E.D., D'Antonio, P.,

Rinker, S. and Lynaugh, J.E. (Eds.), *Enduring issues in American nursing*. New York: Springer, pp. 309–333.

Fenski, M. (1971). Copy of a letter to Provost, Nicholas Hobbs, Vanderbilt University sent to Christman by the author. (Christman's personal archives).

Fisli, B.A. (1994). *The history of the Rush University, College of Nursing and the development of the unification model, 1972–1988*. Loyola University, Chicago: Doctoral Thesis.

Fondiller, S.H. (1984). Pattern for unification. *Nursing Mirror*, 159 (15): 23–24.

Fondiller, S.H. (1999). Nursing education in the 1960s: Revolt and reform. *Nursing and Health Care Perspectives*, 20 (4):182–183.

Foreman, M. (1997). Are men taking over the nursing profession? *Contemporary Nurse*, 6 (1): 26–29.

Frances Payne Bolton School of Nursing, Case Western Reserve University Web page: About Frances Payne Bolton. http://www.cwru.edu [Accessed 22 June, 2005]

Georgopoulos, B. and Christman, L. (1990). *The effects of clinical nursing specialization: A controlled organizational experiment*. New York: Edwin Mellen Press.

Griffin, G.J. and Griffin, J.K. (1973). *History and trends of professional nursing, 7th Ed*. St Louis: Mosby.

Halloran, E.J. (1985). Men in nursing. In McCloskey, J.C. and Grace, H.K. (Eds.), *Current issues in nursing*, St Louis: Mosby, pp. 970–978.

Halloran, E.J. and Welton, J.M. (1994). Why aren't there more men in nursing? In McCloskey, J.C. and Grace, H.K. (Eds.), *Current issues in nursing, 4th Ed*, St Louis: Mosby, pp. 684–691.

Hamilton, D. (2001). Constructing the mind of nursing. In Baer, E.D., D'Antonio, P., Rinker, S. and Lynaugh, J.E. (Eds.), *Enduring issues in American nursing*. New York: Springer, pp. 240-261.

Henderson, V. (1978). Letter to Luther Christman. (Christman's personal archives).

Hilton, L. (2001). A few good men. *NurseWeek*, 14 May: 1–4.

Holm, K., Inman, S.L. and Ward, T.L.V. (1997). Critique of Christman on leadership in practice. *Image: Journal of Nursing Scholarship*, 29(2): 31.

Hubbard, W.N. (1965). Letter to Christman regarding three of Christman's articles on nursing. The Luther Christman collection, Howard Gottlieb Research Center, Boston University, Ma.

Jamieson, E.M., Sewall, M.F. and Suhrie, E.B. (1966). *Trends in nursing history: Their social, international, and ethical relationships, 6th Ed.* Philadelphia: W.B. Saunders.

Joint Commission of Accreditation of Healthcare Organizations (2002). *Healthcare at the crossroads: Strategies for addressing the evolving nursing crisis,* pp.1–88.

Kalisch, B.J. and Kalisch, P.A. (1974). *From training to education: The impact of Federal aid on schools of nursing in the United States during the 1940s.* Final Report of NIH Grant NU0043, Ann Arbor: Minnesota. (Quoted in Merrill, 1998: 56)

Kalisch, P.A. and Kalisch, B.J. (1995). *The advance of American nursing, 3rd Ed.* Philadelphia: J.B. Lippincott.

King, S. (1965). Letter to the Editor. *American Journal of Nursing* 65(9): 77-78.

Ku, R.J. (1985). A challenge to nursing: Eliminating anti-male sexism in American society. In McCloskey, J.C. and Grace, H.K. (Eds.), *Current issues in nursing,* St Louis: Mosby, pp. 979–978.

Lagermann, E.C. (Ed.) (1983). *Nursing history: New perspectives, new possibilities.* New York: Teachers College Press.

Lewenson, S.B. (1996). *Taking charge: Nursing, suffrage and feminism in America, 1873–1920.* New York: NLN Press.

Lewis, M.C. (1998). Men in nursing: A time for re-evaluation. *Interaction*: 9–11.

Lorber, J. (1984). *Women physicians: Careers, status, and power.* New York: Tavistock.

Lusk, B., Russell, R.L., Rodgers, J. & Wilson-Branett, J. (2001). Preregistration nursing education in Australia, New Zealand, the United Kingdom, and the United States of America. *Journal of Nursing Education,* 40 (5):197–202.

Lynaugh, J.E. & Brush, B.L. (1996). *American nursing: From hospitals to health systems.* Cambridge, Massachusetts: Blackwell

Lynaugh, J.E. (2001). Nursing's history: Looking backward and seeing forward. In Baer, E.D., D'Antonio, P., Rinker, S. and Lynaugh, J.E. (Eds.), *Enduring issues in American nursing.* New York: Springer, pp. 10–24.

Lysaught, J.P (1981). *Action in affirmation: Toward an unambiguous profession of nursing.* A Longitudinal Follow-up on the Recommendations of the National Commission for the Study of Nursing and Nursing Education. New York: Mc-Graw-Hill.

Lysaught, J.P. (1978). Christman present: an interview on a life's career in nursing leadership. In Lysaught, J.P. (Ed.), *A Luther Christman anthology.* Nursing Digest Contemporary Publication.

Lysaught, J.P. (Ed.) (1978). *A Luther Christman anthology.* Nursing Digest Contemporary Publication.

MacPhail, J. (1996). Men in nursing. In Kerr, J.R. and MacPhail, J., *Journal of Canadian nursing: Issues and perspectives, 3rd Ed.* St Louis: Mosby, pp. 75-81.

Maggs, C. (Ed.) (1987). *Nursing history: The state of the art.* London: Croom Helm.

Marquis, B., Lillibridge, J. and Madison, J. (1993). Problems and progress as Australia adopts the bachelor's degree as the only entry to practice. *Nursing Outlook,* May/June: 135–140.

McCeland, H. (1952) Reference letter for Christman titled 'To whom it may concern' in the Luther Christman collection, Howard Gottlieb Research Center, Boston University, Ma.

McCloskey, J.C. (1981). Nursing accreditation: To what end? In McClosky, J.C. and Grace, H.K. (Eds.) *Current issues in nursing,* London: Blackwell Scientific Publications (pp. 359–372).

McCullian, E.V. (1935). School Principal's reference letter titled 'To whom it may concern' in the Luther Christman collection, Howard Gottlieb Research Center, Boston University, Ma.

Mellish, J.M. (1990). *A basic history of nursing, 2nd Ed.* Durban: South African Butterworth.

Melosh, B. (1982). *"The physician's hand": Work, culture and conflict in American nursing.* Philadelphia: Temple University Press.

Merrill, S.E. (1998). *Luther Christman: Professional reformer.* Doctoral thesis, University of Michigan, Michigan.

Moore, R.J. (1965). Letter to the editor. *American Journal of Nursing,* 65(4): 53.

Mottus, J.E. (1981). *The New York Nightingales: The emergence of the nursing profession at Bellevue and New York Hospital 1850–1920.* Ann Arbor: UMI Research Press.

Nadig, G.K. (1952). Reference for Luther Christman from the Adviser, Department of Nursing, Temple University, December 1. Luther Christman collection, Howard Gottlieb Research Center, Boston University, Ma.

National Commission for the Study of Nursing and Nursing Education (1970). *An abstract for action* by Jerome P. Lysaught. New York: McGraw-Hill.

National Commission for the Study of Nursing and Nursing Education (1973). *An abstract into action* by Jerome P. Lysaught. New York: McGraw-Hill.

Nichols, E.F. (1997). Educational patterns in nursing. In Chitty, K.K. (Ed.), *Professional nursing: Concepts and challenges, 2nd Ed*. Philadelphia: W.B. Saunders, pp. 33–58.

Pennsylvania School of Nursing for Men, Philadelphia (1939). *Maltesan*. Published in honor of the Founders of the School by the graduating class of 1939.

Perkins, J.L., Bennett, D.N. and Dorman, R.E. (1993). Why men choose nursing. *Nursing and Health Care*, 14(1): 34-38.

Pittman, E. (1985). Goodbye, Florence: The nurses' struggle for status has ended the age of Florence Nightingale. *Australian Society*, February: 8–10.

Porter, E. (1963). Traditions and realities. In Money and Nursing, a special supplement, *American Journal of Nursing*, 63, (11): M-3–M-7.

Porter, S. (1995). *Nursing's relationship with medicine: Critical realist ethnography*. Aldershot, UK: Ashgate Publishing.

Reverby, S.M. (1987). *Ordered to care: The dilemma of American nursing, 1850-1945*. Cambridge: Cambridge University Press.

Roberts, J.I., and Group, T.M. (1995). *Feminism and nursing: An historical perspective on power, status, and political activism in the nursing profession*. Westport, Connecticut: Praeger.

Roberts, M.M. (1954). *American nursing: History and interpretation*. New York: Macmillan.

Schorr, T.M. and Kennedy, M.S. (1999). *100 Years of American nursing: Celebrating a century of caring*. Philadelphia: Lippincott.

Schorr, T.M. and Zimmerman, A. (1988). *Making choices, taking chances: Nurse leaders tell their stories*. St Louis: Mosby.

Schwirian, P. and Moloney, M.M (1998). *Professionalization of nursing: Current issues and trends, 3rd Ed.* Philadelphia: Lippincott

Skivington, S. and Dawkes, D. (1988). Fred Nightingale. *Nursing Times*, 84: 49–51.

Snodgrass, M.E. (1999). *Historical encyclopedia of nursing.* Santa Barbara, California: ABC-CLIO, Inc.

Streubert, H.J. (1994). Male nursing students' perceptions of clinical experience. *Nurse Educator*, 19:28–32.

Sullivan, E. (2002). In a woman's world. *Reflections on Nursing Leadership, Honor Society of Nursing, Sigma Theta Tau International,* Third Quarter: 10–17).

Sutherland, D, (1963). Money at the bedside. In. Money and Nursing, a special supplement, *American Journal of Nursing*, 63(11): M-7–M-12.

Unnamed Author (1998). Letter to Aspen Publishers regarding the publication of collected papers of Luther Christman. Dated 31 July. (Christman's personal archives).

Urban Health (1980). Primary Nursing at Rush-Presbyterian-St. Luke's Hospital.

Walsh, M.R. (1977). *Doctors wanted: No women need apply: Sexual barriers in the medical profession 1835–1975.* New Haven: Yale University Press.

Williams, C. (1992). The glass escalator: Hidden advantages for men in "female" professions. *Social Problems*, 39: 253–267.

Williams, C. (1995). *Still a man's world: Men who do women's work.* Berkeley: University of California Press.

ISBN 1412068339-9

9 781412 068338